A New Color for
Christmas

JON HUNTZINGER, PHD

A New Color for
Christmas

AN ADVENT DEVOTIONAL

   TKU PRESS

A New Color for Christmas
Copyright © 2018 by Jon Huntzinger

Revised edition. *Orange Christmas* was originally published by The Focus
Media Group in 2013.

ISBN: 978-1-945529-49-8 paperback
ISBN: 978-1-945529-50-4 eBook

We hope you hear from the Holy Spirit and receive God's richest blessings
from this book by Gateway Press. We want to provide the highest quality
resources that take the messages, music, and media of Gateway Church to the
world. For more information on other resources from Gateway Publishing,
go to gatewaypublishing.com.

Gateway Press and TKU Press, imprints of Gateway Publishing
700 Blessed Way
Southlake, Texas 76092
gatewaypublishing.com

18 19 20 21 22   7 6 5 4 3 2 1
Printed in the United States of America

To my parents,
Gene and Marion Huntzinger,
who celebrate Christmas well.

Contents

Foreword

I'VE THOUGHT FOR quite some time that God speaks in color. All you have to do is look at tonight's sunset, this morning's dewy garden, winter's sparkling white, autumn's hazy crimson and gold, spring's fresh leaf green, and summer's brilliant ocean blue. God could have made the world gray, but He didn't. He made a glorious, color-filled world for us to enjoy!

The Bible is full of color, too. From Rahab's red cord (Joshua 2:18), to Joseph's coat of many colors (Genesis 37:3), to Lydia's business of selling purple cloth (Acts 16:14), to green pastures (Psalm 23:2), to the white garments of the saints (Revelation 3:5, 7:9), Scripture describes colorful people, colorful worship, and colorful circumstances.

Yes, God speaks in color! And He wants to talk to you this Christmas about the color *orange*. Orange may not be the color Christmas immediately brings to your mind, but in this book you will find that when you allow God to step into the picture of your life, everything speaks of Him.

Even orange.

My journey with this color began a few years after my husband's death. I had never liked orange. In fact, I had been heard to say, "I like every color *except* orange." Suddenly, I found it popping up everywhere. And I liked it! (And yes ... I even started decorating my Christmas trees in red, orange, and copper!) As time went by I realized this "new" color had become indicative of my new life—filled with brightness, warmth, and vibrancy. How interesting then, when in conversation with a psychologist friend at church, I learned that orange is, psychologically speaking, the *color of change*.

Imagine my further surprise when Jon Huntzinger told me about the book he was writing about orange and Christmas. At first glance, these two words don't seem to go together; however, the first Christmas was filled with change.

A girl said *yes* to a miracle, and her life was never the same. A young man said *yes* to protecting that miracle, and he accepted a new responsibility. Together, this couple said *yes* to an unlikely place for a birth, along with the accompanying discomfort and humility. Shepherds said *yes* to obeying an angel choir's rejoicing and left all to go to the manger. Wise men said *yes* to following a star in search of a King, risking the wrath of another king to do so.

And the biggest change of all: *The creative Word of God left heaven and became part of creation* ...

> The One who had flung the stars across the
> galaxies ...
> The One who laid the cornerstone of each
> continent ...
> The One who intimately knew each blossom,
> each snowflake, each grain of sand ...
> *came to walk among us so that He could have*
> *relationship with us.*

But it required a willingness to change. And orange is the color of change.

That's what this book is about—*preparing for change*! Orange will change you. Christmas will change you. May you embrace this book as a gift that will make this Christmas like no other. Prepare to be changed more and more into the likeness of His dear Son, Jesus Christ.

Rebecca Hayford Bauer

Introduction

The Color of Christmas

WHAT IS THE color of Christmas? For many, the answer is red. They may choose cardinal red, fire-engine red, or cherry red—the shade doesn't matter, as long as it's some form of red. People string their trees with red bulbs and adorn the branches with red ornaments. They plaster their homes with red lights. They place red caps on their heads and wear red stockings on their feet. They treat themselves to red-and-white candy canes and use enough red food coloring in their baked goods to turn the Mississippi River pink. Everywhere you look—red. Santa Claus wears a red coat, and his reindeer follow a newcomer with a glowing red nose. Yes, for many people, red is the color of Christmas.

Others think green is the right color. It is the color of Christmas trees, holly, and mistletoe—the natural varieties, at least. Green is the color of Will Ferrell's Christmas jacket in the movie *Elf*, and it is the color of

Dr. Seuss' infamous Grinch, who detests the fabulous festivities of the Whos down in Whoville. Without a doubt, we think of red and green as the colors of Christmas, although I could probably make a case for silver and gold and maybe even white or blue.

Is it even possible to make room on the Christmas palette for orange? For most of us, orange is decidedly *not* a Christmas color. We may like it well enough, but our minds don't associate it with this holiday. During the Christmas season, most of us have left orange far behind. We remember it as the color of Halloween or one of the colors of Thanksgiving. Orange is the color of jack-o'-lanterns and autumn leaves. We associate it with the end of warm weather, the final flash or blaze of glory imprinted on our memories as we wait for the bright pastels of spring. In the coldest months, we find cheer in the shiny and celebratory colors of red and green that light up the "bleak midwinter."[1]

If we haven't left orange behind with the passing of fall, then we associate it with symbols of caution. Orange safety cones cordon off lanes, and road construction crews wear orange vests as they fill

---

1. This expression is known to many through the Christmas gospel song, "In the Bleak Midwinter." My favorite rendition is performed by The Blind Boys of Alabama on their album, *Go Tell It on the Mountain.*

potholes and repair streets. Orange-vested school crossing guards remind us that children may walk in front of our vehicles at any moment. And orange caution signs alert us to drive slowly.

Orange can be one of the colors of a school or our favorite sports team, making it a source of pride. It becomes part of our group identity as we root for our chosen team. Even so, our minds probably don't put the color orange together with Christmas.

Orange is not even one of the primary hues of the color wheel—those colors are red, blue, and yellow. Instead, orange is a secondary color that falls between yellow and red on the color chart. Most color charts contain numerous basic colors and tens of thousands of other hues, all determined by the effects of electromagnetic wavelengths of light on the eye.[2] If the vibration of an object's electrons is the same as that of a light wave, then the light wave will be absorbed and the rest reflected. This is why a red rose looks almost black under a red light. The colors we see are actually the electromagnetic waves of light reflected away from objects. As Victoria Finlay explains, "The best

2. This is the assessment of Pantone, the largest color identification company in the world. See Victoria Finlay, *Color: A Natural History of the Palette* (New York: Random House Trade Paperbacks, 2004), 393–94.

way ... of understanding this is to think not so much of something 'being' a color but of 'doing' a color."[3]

With that said, many of us don't like what orange *does*. Jill Morton of colormatters.com says that orange is "polarizing," meaning people either love it or hate it.[4] They are seldom indifferent to it. This is because color has emotional and psychological meaning in addition to its physical qualities. We can see the evidence of this claim through our common association of certain colors with specific emotions and attitudes. For example, if we say we are feeling "blue," we mean we are feeling sad, discouraged, or depressed. Some people say that they're "green," which means they give special attention to their natural environment. Thus, many people, including the early twentieth-century abstract artist Wassily Kandinsky, regard color as a type of language that speaks to our emotions. They say orange represents health, change, adventure, and assertiveness while it also speaks of separation and restlessness.

Not everyone agrees with this assessment, though. Color historian and scientist Philip Ball dismisses such color-emotion connections, saying, "There can

3. Finlay, 6. See pages 4–8 for an easy-to-understand explanation of the physical nature of light and color.
4. Accessed www.colormatters.com on 25 September 2017.

be no consensus about what colors 'mean' or how to use them 'truthfully.'" He says the association of color with emotion and meaning is an "individual quest."[5] It all depends on personal tastes and interests. If Ball is right and individual interpretation is allowed, then I believe orange is the language of Christmas, and it speaks to the truths of humility, generosity, mystery, possibility, and destiny.

———————

These 25 devotionals are here to help you walk through the wonderful opportunities for change you may encounter this Christmas season. I draw from my own experiences and memories as well as my reflections and studies of the Christmas story in the Bible. I have grouped them according to the Christmas truths mentioned above. Taken together, you will see how they declare the meaning of Christmas and give all of us reasons to rejoice in the precious gift of God's Son.

5. Philip Ball, *Bright Earth: Art and the Invention of Color* (Chicago: University of Chicago Press, 2003), 23.

Part One

Humility

Day 1

Oranges in Old Socks

Born in the likeness of men.
—Philippians 2:7

MY DAD GRADUATED in 1963 from Gordon-Conwell
Seminary near Boston, Massachusetts. He and my
mom soon moved to Kingsport, Tennessee, a north-
eastern town along the North Carolina state line,
to pastor the small congregation of Reedy Creek
Presbyterian Church. This small-town church in the
Appalachian foothills was a humble place for my young
parents to begin their pastoral ministry, but it was also
a good place to raise their young family.

A small-town pastor often serves as the congregation's handyman; he or she does a little of everything.
My dad preached sermons, taught Sunday School,
wrote bulletin announcements, made pastoral house
visits, counseled people through their problems,
officiated weddings and funerals, christened and

baptized, served as a general fix-it man, and occasionally delivered groceries. While he did all these things, my mom raised three, soon-to-be four, children and stretched the $400 per month salary to pay bills, buy food, fill the car with gas, and keep everybody clothed and warm. Our bank account didn't have much left at the end of each month.

Even so, we never went hungry. In fact, we ate the same foods most families like ours did in those days: casseroles, hamburger and hot dog dishes, and peanut butter and jelly or bologna and mustard sandwiches. Quite often my mom served macaroni and cheese covered with bread crumbs and tomato slices, or macaroni and tuna fish with diced celery, or macaroni with hamburger and canned tomatoes. We must have eaten bags and bags of elbow macaroni as we washed it all down with pitchers of Kool-Aid.

At breakfast, we usually drank Tang, ate toast with cinnamon-sugar icing, and instead of serving dry cereal, Mom would break up slices of white bread and put the pieces into a bowl with milk and sugar. We had some fresh fruit like apples and plums in season, but we didn't eat very many berries or bananas. To save money, we seldom ate any beef besides hamburger, and we never ate steak. I consumed countless fish sticks. However, on special days like Christmas, we celebrated with a roasted turkey.

When I was seven years old, my mom put stockings out on Christmas morning. Since our house didn't have a fireplace, she took old rayon socks my dad no longer wore and laid them on the sofa by the tree. We weren't allowed to open presents until we had eaten breakfast and read the Christmas story, but we were allowed to look in our individual Christmas socks. Today, people put out huge Christmas stockings almost as large as Santa's legendary toy bag, which holds a sleigh-full of presents. Sometimes the stockings are hand-woven and covered with snowflakes, teddy bears, or candy canes. My dad's thin black dress socks weren't nearly so big, but Mom stuffed them until they were all out of shape with candy, coloring books, crayons, and other small gifts.

I particularly remember the socks on our first Tennessee Christmas, not because of the candy or presents, but because each contained a single orange. My young mind imagined that oranges must come from faraway, exotic places like *Florida*, where it never snows and the sun shines all the time. That year, before we opened presents or read the Christmas story, we celebrated by eating our oranges. This was the first orange I ever remember eating. It made my fingers sticky and stung my eyes, but it tasted so sweet on my tongue. I decided that I liked it much better than Tang. It was exotic and real, and it came in an old black sock.

Christmas is a reminder that God often gives His greatest gifts in the most common of ways, like when the Savior of all humanity was born to humble parents in a tiny village a few miles from Jerusalem. This shouldn't surprise us, because God has always given His best gifts in this fashion. His gift of freedom for the Israelites came in the form of a fugitive who couldn't speak forcefully or well. God's gift of kingship for Israel came in the form of a shepherd boy with five small stones stuffed into a little bag. And His gift of hope for a new life and a new temple came to a scattered nation in the form of a quirky priest obsessed with cleanliness.

Sometimes we may think God's gifts should come with much pomp and fanfare. We look for fire and listen for thunder. However, salvation did not come in the form of golden chariots with banners flying for all the world to see or with celestial trumpets blaring for all to hear. No, it came quietly in the form of a baby born to simple parents.

The apostle Paul wrote to the believers in the city of Philippi about Jesus: "Though he was in the form of God …[he] emptied himself, by taking the form of a servant, being born in the likeness of men" (Philippians 2:6–7).

Like an orange in an old sock on Christmas morning, eternity manifested itself as a baby laid in a manger. God becoming nothing and being born in our likeness is the perfect example of majesty being found in the mundane. That first Christmas was both extraordinary and ordinary. Most of all, it was real, like my orange. It was much better than Tang.

Day 2

Sweet and Bitter Christmas

A sword will pierce through your own soul.
—Luke 2:35

SOME OF THE specialty foods served during the Christmas season are acquired tastes. Take fruitcake, for instance. When I was young, my mom used to make fruitcake at Christmas. However, I cannot recall ever asking for a second piece! My unrefined palate could not appreciate the combination of candied fruit, chewy nuts, molasses, and rum. I wondered how anyone could eat it and why my mom thought it was so special. I would have preferred something like an ice cream sundae or coconut and chocolate miracle bars with thick vanilla icing.

Another food I couldn't appreciate at the time was sweet and bitter candied orange slices. My mom had learned to make them from her parents. I was suspicious of my grandparents' tastes to begin with, given my grandfather's habit of eating maple syrup like soup from a bowl and his love for sardine sandwiches. The candied oranges only justified my suspicions. I would close my eyes and wince every time my grandfather opened a tin of those finger-sized fish, and I did the same thing whenever I bit through the hard, granulated sugar into those bitter orange rinds.

Like those candied oranges, the first Christmas was both sweet and bitter for young Mary. In the beginning, she tasted sweetness in the greeting of the angel Gabriel: "O favored one, the Lord is with you" (Luke 1:28). She again tasted sweetness in the response of her relative Elizabeth to Mary's pregnancy: "Blessed are you among women, and blessed is the fruit of your womb!" (Luke 1:42). After the birth of her Son, Mary savored the sweetness of the shepherds' visit and their story of the angels' message; she "treasured up all these things, pondering them in her heart" (Luke 2:19).

But there was bitterness, too. When Mary and Joseph took the infant Jesus to be dedicated at the temple in Jerusalem, they met an elderly man named Simeon. Simeon blessed God for the infant, saying Jesus would be the salvation of all people. At first, his words were sweet, but then he declared to Mary, "Behold, this child is appointed for the fall and rising of many in Israel ... and a sword will pierce through your own soul" (Luke 2:34–35). After the amazing word from the angel, the joyous response from Elizabeth, and the exciting news from the shepherds, this disconcerting declaration must have confused Mary. What did this white-haired prophet mean when he said a sword would pierce her heart? Did he not just say that her baby was the One through whom God's revelation to the Gentiles would come?

The image of a sword piercing Mary's heart points to the supremacy of God's Word over her life and over her personal desires and dreams for her Son. Throughout the New Testament, the sword is a symbol of God's Word. When Paul writes to the Ephesians about the sword of the Spirit, he means God's Word, and when the author of Hebrews describes a two-edged sword that discerns the intentions of the heart, he also means God's Word. When John beholds Jesus in glory and sees a two-edged sword coming out of His mouth, he sees Jesus who speaks God's Word (Ephesians 6:17; Hebrews 4:11–12; Revelation 1:16). So when Mary responds to God's promise through the angel and says, "Let it be to me according to your word" (Luke 1:38), she makes herself vulnerable to the sword that God will wield in her life. She says, *Let Your will—not mine—be done in the life of my Son.*

We may find it hard at times to submit to God's Word. Mary surely found it difficult to watch and listen as her Son's fickle friends deserted Him and respected leaders denounced Him. She saw many of Jesus' disciples turn away from Him because He said, "Whoever feeds on my flesh and drinks my blood has eternal life" (John 6:54). Mary heard temple scribes say that her Son was possessed by the devil and out of His mind (Mark 3:22). She saw neighbors and relatives resist Him and cynically ask, "Where did this man get this wisdom and these mighty works? Is not this the carpenter's son? Is not his mother called Mary?" (Matthew 13:54–55). Simeon's words were a precursor of the pain and anguish Mary experienced as she looked upon Roman soldiers nailing her Son to a cross, with their mocking "Hail, King of the Jews!" ringing in her ears (John 6:54, 66; Mark 3:21–22; 6:3; John 8:41; Matthew 27:29).

Yes, I remember those sweet and bitter candied orange peels from my youth. They cause me to pause and wonder what that first Christmas was like for Mary. The sweetness she tasted in the words of the angel Gabriel, her relative Elizabeth, and the shepherds was tinged with bitterness by Simeon's prophecy. She continued to taste that bitterness in the angry responses of many as they spoke harsh words about Jesus. Yet the sweetness of our salvation, described by the elderly Jerusalem prophet, came by

God's Word having dominion in Mary's life, piercing whatever plans she had made for her Son.

Christmas is the season for giving God's Word priority in our lives. Sometimes we discover how difficult it is because it requires us to replace our own treasured desires with His, and the taste of God's Word is often a much stronger flavor than what we're used to. It is like the taste of fruitcake, sardine sandwiches, and candied orange peels to a young boy. Even so, our prayer this Christmas should echo Mary's— *Let Your will be done according to Your Word.* These are the words of salvation. These are the words of Christmas.

Day 3

Mary's Yes

Let it be to me according to your word.
—Luke 1:38

CHRISTMAS BEGAN WHEN a young Jewish girl said *yes* to God's questions: *Do you believe what I have said to you? Do you believe that you are favored and that I can use you to bring change to the world? Do you believe that through you the throne of King David will be established forever?*

Mary affirmed, "Yes, I believe," when she said, "I am the servant of the Lord; let it be to me according to your word" (Luke 1:38). At Christmas, we celebrate this response of faith to the limitless promise implicit in God's question.

Mary was only a girl when the angel Gabriel appeared to her. In today's culture, we would say she was only a child—not a toddler, of course, but a young teenager. We think of Mary as simple and sweet and the very last person any of us would expect God to visit with an angel; we have our own ideas about who is deserving of such grand favors. We think God only gives those blessings to the truly great ones among us, and we have exalted notions of greatness just as the people did during the time of Jesus.

Matthew's Gospel records an incident that illustrates this kind of thinking. After Jesus' transfiguration on the mountain, the disciples argued about who was the greatest (Matthew 17:1–13; 18:1–4). More than likely, they debated who was the greatest among the three figures that James, John, and Peter saw on the mountain—was it Moses, Elijah, or Jesus?

Which of the disciples believed Moses was the greatest? Was it James? Moses had a claim to be the greatest since God had called him to lead Israel out of Egypt. Moses stood up to Pharaoh and the Egyptian army, and God used him to part the Red Sea. God also appeared to him in the midst of a burning bush, fed him with bread from heaven, and gave him tablets inscribed with God's very own words. Furthermore, Scripture says that God spoke to him face-to-face, unlike any other human being had experienced. And Moses' face was so bright with the brilliance of God's glory that he had to wear a veil in order not to blind the other Hebrews. Liberator, Pathfinder, Manna-minister, Law-giver, Glory-reflector. "Moses certainly is the greatest in God's kingdom!" James may have thought.

Who chose Elijah? Was it John? Elijah had a claim to be the greatest as well. He stood against almost 1,000 of Baal's priests, prophets, and Asherah[1] even as he stood up to the apostate king Ahab. God's miraculous provision of food to Elijah under the broom tree was as great as the manna the Lord sent Moses in the wilderness, and God passed by Elijah in a mountain cave just as He did to Moses on the mountainside. Elijah also raised a young boy from death and called fire down from heaven, proving there is only one God. At the end of his ministry, Elijah was last seen rocketing skyward in God's chariot of fire. Most remarkable of all, however, was that God spoke to Elijah in "a low whisper" (1 Kings 19:12). So intimate was his relationship with God and so close was God to Elijah that all the Lord needed to do was whisper for His prophet to hear Him. "Perhaps Elijah is the greatest," John may have thought.

Which of the disciples said Moses wasn't the greatest and neither was Elijah? Who said Jesus was the greatest? Perhaps it was Peter. Jesus fed the multitudes as Moses had and raised the dead to life as Elijah had. Jesus' wisdom was as great as that of

---

1. Asherah (plural, Asherim) were wooden posts or poles that stood near the altars of the Canaanite gods, such as Baal. They were forbidden in the Law of Moses (Deuteronomy 16:21).

Israel's teacher, and His miracles were as wondrous as those of Israel's prophet. Jesus had walked on water, healed the sick, and cast out demons. But more than this, He had accepted Peter's confession that He was "the Christ, the Son of the living God" (Matthew 16:16).

When Jesus came down from the mountain and found His disciples debating these things, His response likely confused them as much as it causes us to wonder now. Jesus put a child in their midst and said, "Whoever humbles himself like this child is the greatest in the kingdom of heaven" (Matthew 18:4). Saying a humble child is the measure of greatness in God's sight is like saying a California cutie—a small orange many of us enjoy eating at Christmastime—is the main course of our holiday dinner. This small citrus fruit may be juicy and sweet, but it cannot compare to rib roast with horseradish dressing or roasted turkey with herb stuffing and cranberry garnish. Yet Jesus says the greatest among us must possess childlike humility. And what is humility? It is responsiveness to God's Word.

Mary heard and accepted the words of the angel. She exulted in the One who would raise her up and do great things: "My spirit rejoices in God my Savior, for he has looked on the humble estate of his servant" (Luke 1:47–48).

Greatness is not measured by how many words from God we hear. It is not determined by how many visions we see or how many miracles God performs through us. Greatness in God's kingdom has nothing to do with politics or power or prestige. It isn't bequeathed to us because we have stood on the mountain like Moses or called fire down from the sky like Elijah. Instead, it has everything to do with our willingness to hear and act upon the words God speaks to us.

When Mary said *yes* to the angel, she responded with childlike humility—*like the child she was*—to the Word of God and gave an example for how we are to celebrate Christmas today. The greatest act of Christmas devotion is for you to say *yes* to the word God is speaking to your heart and see the great things God will do in your life.

Day 4

God's Christmas Smile

*Glory to God in the highest, and on earth
peace among those with whom he is pleased!*
—Luke 2:14

MY BROTHER'S BIRTHDAY is the week before
Christmas. His hair is now white, but when he was
young, it was bright red (although it looked orange to
me). As hard as my parents tried to make his birthday
stand out from Christmas with a cake and a party,
it was inevitably overwhelmed by the avalanche of
Christmas. Cards arrived daily in the mail, carols
played on the stereo, and excitement built in our home
for Christmas Day. My brother never complained
about his mid-December birthday, though; he seemed
to enjoy what he interpreted to be an early start to
opening Christmas presents.

We were living near Washington, D.C., when my
brother had a glimpse of what the first Christmas night

was like for the shepherds who saw a host of angels in the sky over Bethlehem. Our family learned about this during dinner one evening when the topic of conversation turned to heaven. My sister had said that heaven sounded boring with all its gold streets, baby-faced cherubs, and harp music. But my brother responded that heaven wasn't boring at all because the angels there were so beautiful. My dad asked how he knew they were beautiful. My brother replied, "Because I have seen some." He began to tell us that he had been having frightening dreams, to which he responded by doing something he had learned in an after-school Bible program. He recited Bible verses and asked for the blood of Jesus to cover him.

When my brother did this, angels appeared to him. He followed this same practice for several nights. On the first night, an angel with silver hair, wearing a silver sash, appeared and smiled at him. My brother smiled back. Two angels appeared the second night and three angels the third night. Each of the three angels held an object: a book, a stick with leaves, and what appeared to be a handful of flowers. On the fourth night, my brother dreamed of a skeleton, but when he prayed again and asked that the blood of Jesus protect him, the ceiling seemed to disappear, and the sky filled with angels, all of whom were smiling upon him. There were so many that he couldn't count them all. After that, he had no more dark dreams and no more visions of angels. The Lord had comforted a young boy with a vision not unlike the one He gave to young shepherds 2,000 years earlier.

On the first Christmas night, God smiled upon a fearful and suspicious world when one of His angels appeared to the shepherds and said,

> "Fear not, for behold, I bring you good news of great joy that will be for all the people. For unto you is born this day in the city of David a Savior, who is Christ the Lord" (Luke 2:10–11).

Like many of us today, the shepherds lived in a world plagued with all kinds of fears. They feared the Romans, their legions, and their deadly javelins. They feared drought and famine, hardship and hunger. They feared Samaritans who worshipped at another temple and zealots who stirred up trouble and dissension. They feared that God's promises through the prophets would never come to pass and that the future held no hope. They even feared God's wrathful judgment upon sin.

In the midst of all these fears, the angels joyfully declared: "Glory to God in the highest, and on earth peace among those with whom he is pleased!" (Luke 2:14). They sang the same words that the baby they praised would speak years later to His disciples on the day of His resurrection: "Peace be with you" (John 20:19, 21). The disciples need not fear. Jesus was alive, and so too were their hopes and dreams. God was smiling on them.

The apostle Paul uses the word *peace* to describe the entirety of Jesus and His ministry: "For he [Jesus] himself is our peace, who has made us both one and has broken down in his flesh the dividing wall of hostility ... that he might create in himself one new man" (Ephesians 2:14–15). The Ephesian believers did not need to fear separation from God, and neither do we— Jesus has joined us to His Father and brought us near to His ancestral people. This word of peace means we have not been left alone to face our fears. God has drawn close to us and shares in our struggles and aspirations.

God smiled upon the whole world that first Christmas when His angels sang an aria of peace. He smiled upon the shepherds when He announced His presence to them and said, "Fear not." God smiled upon my brother, a little boy frightened by scary dreams, when He sent not one or two or three but a sky full of angels to comfort him. And He smiles upon us this Christmas with words of peace. God knows our fears and the things that keep us awake at night. He says *peace*. Christmas is the season for hearing His words of comfort—*Fear not*—and for seeing His comforting smile in His Son Jesus.

Day 5

Lower than Angels

You have made him a little lower than the heavenly beings.

—Psalm 8:5

ONE CHRISTMAS I got up at 3:30 am to deliver the morning edition of *The Washington Post* to the 175 subscribers on my route. I put on my coat, scarf, and cap and lifted my orange-strapped canvas newspaper bag over my shoulders. Feeling really low, I wondered if anyone else besides Santa and his elves was up this early on Christmas morning. Did people really read the newspaper on Christmas Day? Did they care if I delivered it or not? I really doubted it. I wanted to complain but said a prayer of thanks instead because it was Christmas. For the next several hours, I ran from house to house over frost and ice tossing papers onto porches. Several months later, to my surprise, I was rewarded with a trip to New York City for managing my paper route well. And as I stood on the Empire State Building's observatory deck, I felt as if I was on top of the world.

King David wonders as he thinks about Adam's place in God's creation:

> What is man that you are mindful of him, and the son of man that you care for him? Yet you have made him a little lower than the heavenly beings and crowned him with glory and honor (Psalm 8:4–5).

David perceives Adam and his descendants as lower than the angels who serve God in heaven above while humans remain on earth below. Although they are on earth, God has given humans the high responsibility to rule over His world. Thus, David says about Adam, "You have given him dominion over the works of your hands; you have put all things under his feet" (Psalm 8:6). How will Adam rule? David answers *through the words that he speaks*—"Out of the mouth of babes and infants you have established strength" (Psalm 8:2)—and *through the works that he does.* The speech that forms when we are only infants is God's perfect way to manifest His power against His enemies and to demonstrate the greatness of His rule over the world.

When the author of Hebrews recalls this psalm, he says God preserved this rule for Adam through His

Son Jesus who, like Adam, was made lower than those wondrous angels that fly around His throne, crowned with God's glory (2:5–18). The author also says that this same Jesus is the founder of our salvation, having shared in our own flesh and blood. Beginning with His cries as a baby born in Bethlehem—*out of the mouth of babes and infants you have established strength*—and concluding with His cries as a condemned man at Golgotha, Jesus manifested His Father's greatness and overthrew all His enemies and ours, returning rule over God's marvelous creation to His people.

Even though God created Adam lower than the angels, He sent Jesus into the world so that Adam might retain the high place as ruler over God's creation. God's desire is that His people stand atop His world in faithful and loving stewardship of it. Marvel this Christmas at the radiance of God's angels who sing, "Glory to God in the highest" and wonder at their worship around His throne. Thank God that He cares for us and has restored to us the privilege of ruling over His world through His Son. Most of all, join with the host of heaven in praising God's goodness in everything we do as we worship the Son of God, who in his cries as a baby and dying groans as a man proved He is the Alpha and Omega, the First and the Last, the Highest and the Lowest!

Part Two

Generosity

Day 6

Secret Giving

*When you give to the needy, do not let your left
hand know what your right hand is doing.*
—Matthew 6:3

OUR MODERN-DAY SANTA CLAUS traces his origin to
St. Nicholas of Myra, a fourth-century bishop known
for his good works. According to one account, medieval
nuns in France began the practice of giving oranges
and other small gifts on the eve of St. Nicholas Day to
needy families in honor of the saint's generous gift-
giving.[1] Many people today continue the tradition of
giving each other oranges in memory of the small bags
of gold coins St. Nicholas once gave to an impoverished
family facing desperate circumstances.

1. William J. Bennett, *The True Saint Nicholas: Why He Matters to
Christmas* (New York: Howard Books, 2009), 83.

The traditional story recounts that a father without any money for dowries for his three daughters made the unthinkable decision to sell them into slavery so they would have a place to live and food to eat. Nicholas heard of the family's plight, so he secretly visited their house one night and left a small bag of gold coins inside a window. When the father discovered the bag the next morning, he was overjoyed because it meant that one of his daughters would be spared a life of slavery. Not long after, Nicholas did the same for the second daughter and then for the third.

Nicholas did not give his gifts in public or seek recognition. When he gave the bags of gold, he didn't advertise his generosity or draw attention to his benevolence. He didn't go in the middle of the day with assistants who would recount his acts of goodness for others to hear. There were no scribes present to record the emotional responses of the father and his daughters over their mysterious good fortune. Instead, Nicholas went by himself in the middle of the night and gave in secret.

By giving his gift in secret, Nicholas followed the example Jesus taught His disciples. Time after time, according to Mark's Gospel, Jesus told those He touched and healed to say nothing about Him. When Jesus healed a leper, for instance, Mark reports that He "sternly charged" the man and said, "See that

you say nothing to anyone, but go, show yourself to
the priest and offer for your cleansing what Moses
commanded" (Mark 1:43–44). Later Jesus raised
a young girl from death and "strictly charged" her
parents not to tell others about it (Mark 5:35–43).
And after Jesus restored sight to a blind man, He
commanded the man not to return to his village to tell
his neighbors about it (Mark 8:22–26).[2]

Nicholas knew these stories, and he knew Jesus'
teaching from the Sermon on the Mount. This teaching
provides instructions on giving and warns us to
"beware" of giving simply to be noticed by others.
Those who give with a motivation for recognition will
not be rewarded by God because they will have already

2. Biblical scholars describe these admonitions by Jesus as Mark's
"Messianic Secret," which reminds us that we cannot under-
stand Jesus' healings and exorcisms apart from His ultimate
sacrifice on the cross. New Testament scholar R.T. France
comments, "Secrecy is not an issue in itself. It is rather a
function of the nature of Jesus' message and ministry, which ...
runs counter to conventional human values. The constant
misunderstandings even on the part of Jesus' closest disciples
vividly illustrate the basis for Jesus' caution about allowing
people, even disciples, to talk openly about the [*mustērion*]
which only divine revelation could unveil to human insight."
The Gospel of Mark, The New International Greek Testament
Commentary (Grand Rapids/Cambridge: Eerdmans/Carlisle:
The Paternoster Press, 2002), 31–32.

received the reward of people. They will not receive two rewards. Jesus says, "When you give to the needy, sound no trumpet before you ... do not let your left hand know what your right hand is doing, so that your giving may be in secret. And your Father who sees in secret will reward you" (Matthew 6:2–4). We are to be satisfied with God's approval and blessing.

How hard it is to give in secret! Our human nature desires to get credit for the good things we do and deflect responsibility for the bad. We like the recognition of others, and we enjoy their acclamation. The truth is that we often covet the rewards that come from doing good things. We want the spotlight of attention to shine on us for our generosity. But Jesus says, "Beware." He doesn't say that receiving the appreciation of others is wrong. Rather, He says that our desire for such appreciation should not be the reason we give gifts or do good works. We should give out of love for others. In fact, Jesus tells Nicodemus that love is the motivation behind God's gift of His Son—"For God so loved the world that He gave ..." (John 3:16).

When God gave His Son, He didn't do so by announcing it to emperors, kings, or sheiks. He doesn't need their praise. God didn't send angels to the high priests, philosophers, or oracles of the day. He doesn't need their endorsement. But God did send angels to shepherds in the fields of a small province on the border of the Roman Empire at night.

Today we give oranges as symbols of St. Nicholas' bags of gold coins that he gave in secret to a poor father and his daughters. This small gift of fruit reminds us that when we give as he did, we will receive our reward. We will hear, "Well done, good and faithful servant," and be invited to enter the joy of the Lord (Matthew 25:23). A day will come, Jesus says, when we will be rewarded for the good things we have done for Him. We will be placed at the right hand of God and inherit a kingdom because we have fed, clothed, comforted, and visited Him. If we ask, "When did we do these things for you?" Jesus will answer, *When you gave to those who needed such things* (Matthew 25:34–40). Secret giving is for the benefit of others. St. Nicholas practiced this kind of generosity, but his secret gifts were eventually discovered, just as we have discovered the way God gave the gift of His Son on that first Christmas night.

Day 7

A New Birth of Freedom

For freedom Christ has set us free.
—Galatians 5:1

ONE OF MY favorite Christmas decorations is a Christopher Radko glass ornament. It is fashioned to look like Abraham Lincoln, with light-orange coloration of the president's face. My interest in the sixteenth president began in high school when I first read Stephen Oates' biography, *With Malice Toward None: A Life of Abraham Lincoln.* Lincoln's humble background, perseverance through difficulty, and leadership during the Civil War have inspired me. Of course, his most significant accomplishment was the signing of the Emancipation Proclamation, which was a first step toward the eradication of slavery in 1863 and freedom for all Americans. My Lincoln ornament reminds me of these things.

Freedom is the primary topic of Paul's letter to the church in Galatia, where, incidentally, St. Nicholas would later live. Paul urges the Galatians to hold tight to the gift of freedom that Jesus has given them to worship God apart from the requirements of other peoples' traditions: "For freedom Christ has set us free; stand firm therefore, and do not submit again to a yoke of slavery" (Galatians 5:1). Paul writes these words in response to the attempt of some teachers to convince the Gentile Galatians that their salvation must be validated by keeping the dietary requirements of the Jewish law and by practicing circumcision. These teachers were telling the Galatians that they could protect their newfound freedom by obeying some specific rules, but Paul calls this "slavery."

People tend to like their rituals and traditions and the feelings of familiarity and stability that they bring. And most often, such as when I hang my special Christmas ornament, they do deepen and enrich our experience. Especially at times like Christmas, we like the comfort of old stories and the old ways of doing things. Our rituals assure us that the blessed times of the past can again be experienced when we do the same things in the same ways.

Sometimes, though, we become bound by our rituals. Paul says that Jesus came to give us a "new birth of freedom"—to use Abraham Lincoln's words from the Gettysburg battlefield—from the patterns of the past into a new way of life for the present.[1]

This is why Paul writes:

> When the fullness of time had come, God sent forth his Son, born of woman, born under the law, to redeem those who were under the law, so that we might receive adoption as sons. And because you are sons, God has sent the Spirit of his Son into our hearts, crying "Abba! Father!" (Galatians 4:4–6).

The first Christmas was about God's generosity to us as sons and daughters through the gift of His Son to call Him *Father*.

According to Paul, God gave this gift in the "fullness of time," which means that Christmas is the delivery day of a full-term pregnancy for all people. Just as Jesus was born in the fullness of time after nine months, so also His birth represents a new birth of freedom for those of us who believe in Him to become adopted sons and daughters of God. It is our delivery day from the slavery of old ways of thinking

---

1. See Lincoln's Gettysburg Address, 19 November 1863. For insightful discussion of the address and Lincoln's remarks, read Ronald C. White, Jr., *The Eloquent President: A Portrait of Lincoln through His Words* (New York: Random House, 2005).

and we move into the freedom of new life. And like all newborn babies who loudly cry out at their delivery, we should cry out too, with gratitude and praise, at our entrance into the family of God. With the strong lungs of people who have been given new life by the Spirit, we should shout *Hallelujah*! Christmas is the season to declare our freedom and to cry out that we are sons and daughters of the Most High God. It is the time to say to the world, "We are free!" It is the day to rejoice, "God is our Father!"

Day 8

Commensality Christmas

*For the bread of God is he who comes down
from heaven and gives life to the world.*
—John 6:33

IF WE ARE honest, most of us have experienced the excess of Christmas. We have spent too much money on gifts and done too much shopping. We have drunk too much eggnog or punch and eaten too many chocolate-covered cherries. We have chanted too much "Ho! Ho! Ho!" and sung one too many renditions of "Jingle Bells."

In years past, my wife, Penney, and I would visit her parents for Christmas when they lived in central Florida. One year we drove to the town of Indian River to pick oranges. The air was warm and filled with the scent of salt, sand, and moss, which is so familiar to that part of the country. We spent a beautiful afternoon walking through the groves and picking fruit. I have always loved to eat oranges, and that day I ate one after another. After we had picked enough to fill several baskets, we squeezed some into fresh juice, which I drank on the way home. That night I became sick with citric acid poisoning. I had eaten too many oranges and had drunk too much juice.

Jesus' opponents accused Him of eating and drinking too much during His ministry. On one occasion, He retorted, "John came neither eating nor drinking, and they say, 'He has a demon.' The Son of Man came eating and drinking, and they say, 'Look at him! A glutton and a drunkard, a friend of tax collectors and sinners!'" (Matthew 11:18–19). Of course, unlike me, Jesus didn't make Himself sick by eating or drinking too much. The accusations against Him had nothing to do with gluttony or drunkenness. Instead, they had everything to do with the people to whom Jesus ministered. Jesus ate and drank with tax collectors and sinners, people regarded as unclean because of their association with Gentiles or unworthy because they were too busy or burdened with the cares of life to keep all the laws of the covenant.

To eat and drink with others is to practice *commensality*, which in the ancient world was the primary way that people formed relationships and showed honor to one another. In commensality, the host shows generosity to his guests by providing the best from his pantry and storeroom. He serves his company first and makes sure they have as much as they want, showing his esteem for them.

Jesus practiced commensality everywhere He went by providing for His disciples, the large crowds, and even sinners. All the while, He built relationships with them and showed honor to them. One famous example is when Jesus multiplied loaves and fish and fed more than 5,000 people (Matthew 14:13–21, Mark 6:20–44, Luke 9:10–17, John 6:1–15).[1] He took a small portion of food and, with the help of the disciples, served everyone present. All the people ate and were satisfied. Afterwards, the disciples picked up twelve baskets of leftover food, which served as a sign to them that they would always have what they needed as long as they served others and followed Jesus' example.

Nonetheless, we often overindulge, just as I did at Indian River. We frequently think of ourselves first. Our desires demand to be met, just as our appetites growl if they're ignored. We end up honoring ourselves and forgetting about the needs of others. After we have eaten, sung, danced, laughed, spent, and celebrated, we have little left over to share with others. If we listen carefully, however, Jesus says to us today what He said

1. The feeding of the 5,000 is the only miracle performed by Jesus recorded in all four Gospels.

to the disciples before the miracle of the loaves and fish—"You give them something to eat."

After the feeding miracle, Jesus said, "The bread of God is he who comes down from heaven and gives life to the world. ... I am the bread of life" (John 6:30–35). Jesus is God's bread of commensality for us. His very presence among us is a sign of the honor God has bestowed on us and speaks of His desire to have fellowship with us. It is a sign that He has given His best in Jesus and not withheld anything for Himself.

Christmas is about commensality. It is about the fellowship we have with God and the Bread of Life He has given to us. This year, eat a few less chocolate-covered cherries—and a few less oranges—and extend a few more invitations for others to join you at your table. Honor those around you and give them your very best. Follow our heavenly Father's example and practice a commensality Christmas.

Day 9

A Christmas Autograph

*God has highly exalted him and bestowed on
him the name that is above every name.*
—Philippians 2:9

GIFT CARDS ARE the Christmas present of choice
for many of us these days. They allow us to give the
perfect gift in the perfect color and the perfect size
without having to do any hard work. We don't have to
fight the crowds to find exotic soaps and lotions, books
on obscure topics, his and hers sweaters, or bomber
hats. And yet we lose something when we stop making
and choosing gifts for our loved ones.

Over the years, my daughter has chosen to create
and choose gifts for her family that are full of meaning
and love. Her selections show that she has paid
attention to us and the things we like. One of my
favorite gifts from her is a glass ornament decorated
with orange swirls. She picked it out at a shop in early

autumn one year, and because she had held onto it for several months, it was the first present she gave me to open that Christmas morning.

A couple years earlier, she had burned a CD with many of my favorite Christmas carols and songs. Before that, she gave me an autographed baseball for my birthday. She was seven years old at the time and had overheard me compliment her brother on a ball one of the Los Angeles Dodgers signed at a baseball game for him. She had heard me say that it was a great ball and that I wished I had one like it. She felt bad that I didn't have one for myself, so she took a used baseball from her brother's bag and signed it four times: *Happy Birthday, Dad, Charissa Huntzinger.* She wanted me to have my own signed baseball. It now sits on a shelf behind my desk at home where I can see it every day. I own no possession more valuable to me than that autographed baseball.

The story of the Exodus begins with God giving His name to Israel. When He appears to Moses in the burning bush, He says, "Say this to the people of Israel, 'I AM has sent me to you.' ... This is my name forever" (Exodus 3:14–15). God then signs His autograph to them in the gifts He gives: the manna and quail, the tablets with the commandments, and the light of fire. Jesus so closely identifies with God's *I AM* autograph that He says to His disciples: "*I am* the bread of life ...

I am the light of the world ... *I am* the good shepherd ...
I am the resurrection and the life ... *I am* the way,
the truth, and the life ... and *I am* the vine (of the
branches)" (John 6, 8, 10, 11, 14, 15). Each of these
names directly link Him to the Exodus story: the bread
of life links Jesus to the manna; the light of the world
links Him to the fiery cloud before the people; the good
shepherd links Him to the way God delivered the
people by going before them; the resurrection and the
life links Him to God's purpose for delivering Israel,
which was to replace the death of Egypt with the new
life of Canaan; the way, the truth, and the life links Him
to the commandments given at Sinai; and the vine of
the branches links Him to God's goal for settling Israel
in Canaan, which was to be fruitful for all nations.[1]

Paul has this *I AM* in mind when he writes to
the Philippians and says that Jesus was "born in the
likeness of men" and willingly died on a cross.

---

1. When Jesus says, "I am the way, the truth, and the life," He
   means that He doesn't just point out the way to God or give
   directions for the way—He *is* the way. Since the Torah was
   the way the Israelites were to live and represented God's
   truth to them and life for them, Jesus is telling the disciples
   that He is God's living Torah. (Time after time in the book of
   Deuteronomy, Moses urges the people to walk in the way, by
   which he means that they are to keep the law [5:33; 8:6; 10:12].)
   For this reason, they must be quick to take hold of God's word
   that is being spoken to them in Jesus Himself.

Therefore, God has highly exalted him and bestowed on him the name that is above every name, so that at the name of Jesus every knee should bow, in heaven and on earth and under the earth, and every tongue confess that Jesus Christ is Lord, to the glory of God the Father (Philippians 2:9–11).

Many think the name Paul says is bestowed on Jesus is *Jesus*, but what Paul actually has in mind is God's covenant name.[2] It is the name *I AM* revealed to Moses in the wilderness, and it has now been given to Jesus as His own.

This means that Jesus is God's personal, living autograph to us. God placed His name on His Son and gave Him to us. By giving us such a great gift, God shows how much He has been paying attention to us, how much He loves us, and that Christmas is not just

---

2. See Richard Bauckham, *Jesus and the God of Israel: God Crucified and Other Studies on the New Testament's Christology of Divine Identity* (Grand Rapids/Cambridge: Eerdmans, 2008). He writes, "There can be no doubt that 'the name that is above every name' (v. 9) is YHWH: it is inconceivable that any Jewish writer could use this phrase for a name other than God's own unique name. ... Jesus is given the divine name because he participates in the divine sovereignty. Thus, confession 'that Jesus Christ is Lord' (v. 11) is both a surrogate for calling on him by his name, YHWH, and also a confession of his lordship" (199–200).

a celebration of Jesus' birthday. It is a celebration of our own as well, in which He says over and over to us, *Happy Birthday, Happy Birthday, Happy Birthday, Happy Birthday*!

Day 10

A Toasty Orange Vest

Will he much more clothe you?
—Matthew 6:30

WHEN MY DAUGHTER was young, one of her favorite Christmas stories was *Little Robin's Christmas*.[1] This story centers on a little bird who gives away his collection of seven winter vests to his animal friends the week before Christmas. When he sees that Frog is cold, he gives away his white vest. When he sees that Hedgehog is freezing, he gives away his green vest. To Mole he gives his pink vest; to Squirrel he gives his yellow vest; to Rabbit he gives his blue vest; to Baby Otter he gives his purple vest. On Christmas Eve, the bird sees a shivering mouse and gives away his last vest, a "toasty orange one." Because he has given away

---

1. Jan Fearnley, *Little Robin's Christmas* (Waukesha, WI: Little Tiger Press, 1998).

all his vests, the bird falls asleep cold in the snow.
Later that night he is found by a jolly man in a sleigh
who knows all about his generosity. The jolly man
takes him home where his wife sews a bright red vest
for the small bird.

When Penney and I first gave this book to our
daughter, she made us read it over and over again.
We read it so many times that we all learned it by
heart, and it became a Christmas tradition for many
years. I was more than happy to read the picture book
to my daughter and see her eyes take in the colorful
drawings, knowing that her heart was taking in the
wisdom of the story as well.

The Bible is full of stories of the unusual and
marvelous gifts that God gives to His people. God
gives a son to Abraham when he is one hundred years
old (Genesis 21:1–7). He gives fresh oil to a widow
during a time of famine (1 Kings 17:8–16). He gives
"beauty for ashes" (Isaiah 61:3). And He gives His very
own Spirit with wisdom, understanding, and power to
those who follow after His Son (1 Corinthians 12:4–11).
These stories depict the God of Israel as a generous,
gift-giving God.

Just as God gives gifts, we are to follow His example
and give gifts as well. In the Sermon on the Mount,
Jesus says we must "give to the one who begs from
[us] and do not refuse the one who would borrow from

[us]" (Matthew 5:42). We are to love all people and give prayers on behalf of those who make life hard and difficult for us: "Love your enemies and pray for those who persecute you" (Matthew 5:44).

Not surprisingly, we are to give to the poor. What is surprising, though, is that when we give, we are not to expect any recognition for our benevolence: "When you give to the needy, do not let your left hand know what your right hand is doing, so that your giving may be in secret" (Matthew 6:3–4). Jesus' disciples do not give the way others give.

When Jesus teaches us how to pray, He says we are to forgive, even as we have been forgiven. And what is forgiveness? It's extending mercy when there is repentance. It isn't ignoring sin or avoiding it by saying, "It's alright; forget about it." Forgiveness is giving others the opportunity to be restored despite the wrong they have done. It's the greatest gift we can give to others because it reflects the greatest gift God has given to us.

We are to give because we have received, and it was through a story about a little bird who gives away his last "toasty orange" vest that my daughter, wife, and I were reminded how God gave His Son and His Son gave His life for us. To borrow from the words of the story: Jesus gave away His last orange vest and fell asleep cold in the snow so we might be forgiven of our sins and thus be enabled to forgive others.

This Christmas the Lord wants us to receive the life of Jesus into our own and share it with others. To give and forgive is not always easy; it is often inconvenient, uncomfortable, and sacrificial. But when we give away our very own orange vests, we can be certain that God sees, and He will replace them with red ones. This is why the song of God's gift of salvation, first sung by the angels at the birth of Jesus, will conclude with a final trumpet blast and a Christmas gift for the ages when we exchange our present bodies for glorious new ones. At that trumpet, the apostle Paul says, "The dead will be raised imperishable, and we shall be changed. For this perishable body must put on the imperishable, and this mortal body must put on immortality" (1 Corinthians 15:52–53). Christmas is the season for receiving Jesus' orange vest and giving away our own as we look forward to wearing bright new ones one day.

Part Three

Mystery

Day 11

Our Christmas Pomander Ball

He was pierced for our transgressions;
he was crushed for our iniquities.
—Isaiah 53:5

IN YEARS PAST, my mom made pomander balls and
gave them as Christmas gifts to friends and family.
Pomander balls often consist of oranges covered with
cloves and decorated with ribbon. People place them
in closets, drawers, and trunks to protect clothes from
moths and preserve them for future years.

As a boy, though, I never understood their appeal.
I didn't like the strong scent of the cloves any more
than the moths did. The pomander balls didn't
smell like Christmas to me. They didn't smell like
evergreen trees or burning candles or hot cocoa or
peppermint. Instead, they smelled like the antique
stores my mom and dad liked to visit. And I had to
be careful about how I held them because the cloves

were sharp and would prick my fingers if I grabbed them too tightly.

I wondered at my mom's patience as she made hundreds of small cuts in the peels of the oranges and then pressed the cloves into them. I watched as she took a needle and made tiny incisions in the orange. She began at the top, making the cuts and setting the cloves in a circular fashion. She worked deliberately, careful not to break the cloves when she pressed them into the cuts or when she held them as she worked. She finished by wrapping a thin ribbon once or twice around the orange and then pinned it to the top.

The apostle Matthew tells us that wise men from the east traveled to Bethlehem to see the young child Jesus, although we don't know how many came. It could have been three, according to the well-known carol by John Henry Hopkins, or six or more. We do know that they knelt in worship and presented gifts of gold, frankincense, and myrrh to Jesus. These were uncommon gifts to give to a boy born to humble parents. What did Mary and Joseph think of the myrrh? The brownish-red gum had a strong scent and a bitter taste. It was a costly gift made from a bush cultivated in Arabia and East Africa and was used in ointments and for embalming the dead.

Mary may have kept the myrrh and had it with her when she saw the body of her Son taken down from a Roman cross. Luke says: "The women who had come with him from Galilee followed and saw the tomb and how his body was laid. Then they returned and prepared spices and ointments ... On the first day of the week, at early dawn, they went to the tomb, taking the spices they had prepared" (Luke 23:55–24:1). The myrrh from the wise men may have been one of the spices used by Mary and the women. They were not alone in their desire to give proper care to Jesus' body, for John reports that Nicodemus too brought myrrh to Golgotha to anoint the body before binding it with linen and placing it in the dark tomb (John 19:38–42).

At Christmas, I think of Jesus as our life-preserving pomander ball. Pricked and cut from top to bottom like the orange, He bore our many sins and transgressions. As Isaiah prophesied by faith,

> He was pierced for our transgressions;
> > he was crushed for our iniquities;
> upon him was the chastisement that brought us
> > peace,
> > and with his wounds we are healed (Isaiah 53:5).[1]

---

1. The Hebrew word is *hālal* and is translated in the Greek as *hō mōlōps*, which is used by Peter in his letter when he quotes from Isaiah: "He committed no sin, neither was deceit found in his mouth. When he was reviled, he did not revile in return. ... He himself bore our sins in his body on the tree. ... By his wounds you have been healed" (1 Peter 2:22–24).

Jesus was pierced. His scalp and brow were penetrated by a crown of thorns, His back and legs lacerated by the bits of bone and metal in the leather whips used to scourge Him. His side was stabbed by a Roman spear. And after Jesus' body was pierced, His followers covered it with myrrh and other strong-smelling spices, wrapped it in strips of linen, and laid it in a tomb.

These things happened for our sake. Jesus' perforated and bound body is the sacrifice that protects us from those things that eat at us and destroy us, such as ego, sin, and fear. But the enormity of our ego, the corrosive nature of our sin, and the depth of our fear are often lost on us. We view them as small and insignificant. We insist on having things our way without thinking about how our actions affect others. We don't weigh the impact of our impatient or critical words on family members or friends. Or we refuse to reach out and help others because we're uncertain of what people will think. My father-in-law was fond of an Italian proverb he told numerous times to his nieces, nephews, and grandchildren: "A thousand nothings broke the donkey's back." It is not too much to say that Jesus was pierced and His body was broken like the donkey of the proverb for all of our moth-like nothings.

We are like garments preserved from fabric-eating moths by a Christmas pomander ball. Jesus was

pierced—not just by thorns and whips and spears
but by our own willfulness, carelessness, and fearful-
ness—and His body anointed with spices and wrapped
in linen to preserve us from the destructive conse-
quences of our sins. The good news proclaimed by the
angels over Bethlehem is that He was born to take our
thousand nothings upon Himself and replace them
with a single something: a life of peace, goodwill, and
wholeness with Him. It is a Christmas present for all
eternity.

Day 12

Bonhoeffer's Christmas

They shall call his name Immanuel ...
God with us.

—Matthew 1:23

THE GERMAN PASTOR Dietrich Bonhoeffer was imprisoned by the Nazis and eventually executed in April 1945. Two years earlier, during the Advent season of 1943, he wrote a letter to his parents from prison. Albrecht Altdorfer's sixteenth-century painting, *The Nativity*, was very much on Bonhoeffer's mind at the time. The painting depicts a black sky, large moon, and, most strikingly, an orange brick house in ruins. Its walls are broken down, the ceiling has collapsed, and grass grows all around. Mary, Joseph, and the infant Jesus are alone. There are no shepherds in attendance and no wise men to give gifts. Only cherubic angels look on.

As he thought about the painting's "dilapidated house" and his own situation, Bonhoeffer wrote,

"A more meaningful and authentic Christmas is celebrated here [in prison] by many people than in places where only the name of the feast remains. Misery, pain, poverty, loneliness, helplessness, and guilt have an altogether different meaning in God's eyes than in the judgment of men. God turns toward the very places from which humans tend to turn away."[1]

Bonhoeffer saw in Altdorfer's painting the profound truth of Christmas: God makes Himself present in the most unlikely places. Not only is He present around our decorated trees where we open presents and our sumptuous tables where we enjoy delightful meals, but He also makes Himself present where there are no trees, no tables, no presents, and no meals. We find Him where there is lack, things are lost, and people are lonely.

Altdorfer's depiction of the world into which Jesus was born is far different than the seasonal Hallmark cards we enjoy so much. He portrays the world in a state of disrepair and brokenness. It is not hard to see why the German pastor found encouragement in this painting, given the bleak reality of his own situation.

---

1. *The Mystery of Holy Night*, edited by Manfred Weber and translated by Peter Heinegg (New York: The Crossroad Publishing Company, 1996), 3.

Bonhoeffer wrote about what he knew. Shut off from his family and friends, alone and helpless in a Berlin prison, he experienced God nonetheless right where he was. He experienced Christmas in a place where most people had turned their backs and were intent on ignoring.

The painting Bonhoeffer recalled while in prison reminds us that God is with us wherever we find ourselves. Just as Altdorfer imagined Mary, Joseph, and Jesus in the shambles of a broken-down house, Matthew affirms in his Gospel that God is with us. *Immanuel.* He is with us wherever we are, regardless of the ruins we have made of things or how guilty we might be.

Christmas is a celebration of God turning His face towards a hurting and impoverished world, rather than turning His back on it. It is a celebration that God has not forgotten the lonely, the weak, or the guilty. He has not forgotten us. It is a celebration that God has come to our dilapidated houses to inhabit them and to be with us. Welcome God this Christmas into those places in your life that need repair. Welcome Him into those places of hurt and guilt from which you would rather turn away. When you do, you will discover, as Bonhoeffer would testify, that God has already turned there and is waiting to celebrate Christmas with you.

Day 13

Doornails and Abundant Life

I came that they may have life and have it
abundantly.

—John 10:10

I FOLLOW A personal Christmas tradition of reading
Charles Dickens' *A Christmas Carol* each year in the
orange-colored paperback my aunt gave to me when I was
a young boy. I feel the spirit of the season when I read on
the first page: "Old Marley was as dead as a door-nail."[1]

In times past, nails were driven through a door, and
the nail's protruding end was bent over on the other
side to secure it. This practice added stability to the
various pieces of wood that might make up a door.
However, it also ensured that the nail could never be
used for anything else. Dead. As a doornail.

---

1. Charles Dickens, *A Christmas Carol*, Dover Thrift Editions
   (Mineola, NY: Dover Publications, 1991), 1.

"I might have been inclined, myself, to regard a
> coffin-nail as the deadest piece of ironmongery
> in the trade. But the wisdom of our ancestors is
> in the simile ... You will therefore permit me to
> repeat, emphatically, that Marley was as dead as a
> door-nail."[2]

These words always shake up my complacent ideas about Christmas and remind me that the birth of Jesus is ultimately about cold, hard, and irretrievably bent doornails and God's abundant, everlasting life.

In contrast to his description of Jacob Marley's condition is the one Dickens gives of the Spirit of Christmas Present. When Scrooge opens his bedroom door to see the source of light shining underneath it, he is startled by a laughing apparition. His room has transformed into a banquet hall, and a "jolly Giant" sits upon a mound of meats, fruits, puddings, cakes, and "seething bowls of punch, that made the chamber dim with their delicious steam."[3]

Here Scrooge encounters a being whose life places a question mark over his own. Whereas he eats thin gruel, the Spirit of Christmas Present exults in a thick table of abundance that reaches up to the ceiling of

---

2. *A Christmas Carol*, 1.
3. *A Christmas Carol*, 77.

the room. Scrooge sees that Christmas is for celebration, feasting, and laughter. But he, like so many of us from time to time, chooses commiseration, seclusion, and "bah humbug" instead. Not that we don't have reasons for such feelings and behavior. A tiresome job with difficult and profane co-workers, pernicious poor health, or family matters that refuse to be resolved but seem to become more chaotic and troublesome over time, all provide justification for feeling like Scrooge.

The Spirit of Christmas Present reveals what is possible, however. While the Spirit of Christmas Past reminds Scrooge of what has happened and cannot be changed, and the Spirit of Christmas Yet to Come points to the natural outcome of the choices that he has made, the Spirit of Christmas Present offers hope. This Spirit's abundant feast speaks of the wonderful blessings available to those who grab the hem of Jesus' garment.

Jesus embodies the Spirit of Christmas Present when He says, "The thief comes only to steal and kill and destroy. I came that they may have life and have it abundantly. I am the good shepherd. The good shepherd lays down his life for the sheep" (John 10:10–11).

Jesus has come because there is a thief who wants to hammer us, bend us, and make doornails of our lives. He wants to nail fear into our faith. He wants to drive discouragement into our hopes. He wants to strike anger and bitterness into our love. He wants to hammer death deep within us. But Jesus says, "Life!"

Jesus hasn't come merely to make life bearable. He hasn't come to extend life's status quo. Nor has He come to help us manage life's fears, disappointments, and failures. Jesus has come to give us abundant life that is rich and bountiful and exceeds all our expectations (John 10:10–11, 15, 17, 18). He has come to offer life like that of the Spirit of Christmas Present. Jesus does so by bearing the doornails intended for you and me.

After His teaching about the abundant life, Jesus learns that His friend Lazarus has died. John makes it clear that Lazarus was dead, for Jesus arrives at the tomb four days later (John 11:17). *Dead as a doornail.* At the time, people believed the spirit of a person remained with the body for three days before departing.[4] So when Jesus raised Jairus' daughter to life and did the same for the widow of Nain's son, people marveled at the miracles but likely viewed them as resuscitations (Mark 5:35–43; Luke 7:11–17). Not so here. Lazarus is no more alive than a doornail. The raising of Lazarus is a type of resurrection. It is abundant life.[5]

4. Mishnah, Yebamoth 16.3.
5. Paul prays that the Father of Glory will give the Ephesian believers a spirit of wisdom to know "what is the immeasurable greatness of his power toward us who believe, according to the working of his great might that he worked in Christ when

Jesus was born to bear our doornails, and for this reason, the Spirit of Christmas Present urges us to celebrate life. This year, He desires to bring change to our lives and restore those things that have been stolen from us, lost to us, or have died in us. He wants to fill our lives to the ceiling of our experience. Can we believe it? Are we ready to experience new life like old Scrooge? Let us open the door of Christmas, grab the hem of Jesus' garment, and look upon the abundant life God has prepared for us in Jesus. Let the goodness of the Spirit of Christmas Present bless us this year.

he raised him from the dead and seated him at his right hand in the heavenly places" (Ephesians 1:19–21). It is this power that raised Lazarus and also Jesus from the dead. It is the same power at work when Jesus is conceived and born in Bethlehem. Paul prays that the Spirit of Christmas Present will be given to the Ephesians to bring about a change of understanding of who they are and an awareness of the nature of the power God has released to them. Paul wants them to open their lives to paradigm-shifting, resurrection-lifting change.

Day 14

Betelgeuse and Bethlehem

And the Word became flesh and
dwelt among us.

—John 1:14

THE SINGLE BIGGEST object most of us will ever see
might surprise you. Some will think of a skyscraper
like the Sears Tower in Chicago or a structure like
the Golden Gate Bridge in San Francisco. Others who
have traveled the globe will think of the Great Wall of
China or the Burj Khalifa Tower in the United Arab
Emirates. And yet others will look to the natural world
and say it is the Grand Canyon with its wide expanse,
great depth, and muted colors, or perhaps one of the
great mountains of the world like Denali in Alaska,
Everest in Nepal, or Kilimanjaro in Tanzania. The
truly perceptive among us will look to the sky and say
that the sun is the largest object they will ever see with
their own eyes.

The single biggest object most of us will ever see is a star in the sky, but it's not our sun. In fact, it doesn't seem so large when we look at it. It is a point of light in the constellation Orion with the unusual name *Betelgeuse* (Bee-tle-juice). You don't need binoculars or a small telescope to see it; you just need to know where to look. It is above and to the left of Orion's belt. This single star may be seen from any place on earth except Antarctica, and it shines brightly enough to be seen from within the largest and brightest urban areas. Astronomer Bob Berman puts into perspective the size of Betelgeuse when he writes: "If [Betelgeuse] were an empty jar and we could unscrew its lid to pour in balls the size of our planet at the rate of a hundred a second, we couldn't fill [it] in thirty thousand years."[1] Thirty thousand years? The size of Betelgeuse simply boggles the mind.

Though classified as a red giant, Betelgeuse is really an immense orange sun. Berman explains,

> "Betelgeuse is not really a red star at all. Because it is technically termed a red supergiant, some observers expect it to live up to that title and be as red as a stop light, or at least a glowing ember. But if you could

1. *Secrets of the Night Sky: The Most Amazing Things in the Universe You Can See with the Naked Eye* (New York: William Morrow and Company, 1995), 30.

match Betelgeuse to a color chart at a paint store
you'd find it slightly on the orange side of yellow."[2]

This orange star appears small when seen with
an unaided eye from the earth, and yet it is the
single biggest thing that most of us will ever see. One
Christmas, Penney gave me a small telescope as a
present, and one of the first objects I used it to look at
was Betelgeuse.

The birth of Jesus is the miracle of all miracles,
C.S. Lewis says. He calls it the "Grand Miracle" that
gives meaning to all the other works of God. It exceeds
human imagination that God chose a young girl from
a small people as the means of blessing all nations.
Through a long process of selection that began with
Abraham and continued through the Exodus and later
the exile, God finally decided upon a single girl: "The
process [of redemption] grows narrower and narrower,
sharpens at last into one small bright point like the
head of a spear. It is a Jewish girl at her prayers. All
humanity ... has narrowed to that."[3]

The significance of this "small bright point" is
twofold. The first is that God Himself shows faith

2. *Secrets*, 34–35.
3. C.S. Lewis, *Miracles: A Preliminary Study* (New York:
Touchstone, 1996), 154.

by choosing a girl made in His image to fulfill His purposes. The Creator of the cosmos places the hope of all people throughout all history upon her because He favors her. The second is that this girl believes God chose her. When the angel says that she will conceive and bear a son and "He will be great and will be called the Son of the Most High" (Luke 1:32), Mary grasps that this can happen through her. She believes. When she is all alone and has every reason to doubt herself and dismiss the angel and his message as an incredible fantasy—as apparently Zechariah did when the angel appeared to tell him about the birth of his son John— she agrees that all things are possible with God.

Jesus tells His disciples that faith the size of a mustard seed can move mountains (Matthew 17:20–21). When He says this, He means that it isn't the largeness of our faith that matters but that we believe God wants to act in our lives. Since Jesus earlier compared a mustard seed to the kingdom of heaven, He means faith in God's purposes. Do we trust in Him and His ways? Mary did. The nexus of divine and human faith exemplified that first Christmas may not have moved any mountains, but it did draw heaven down to earth.

Betelgeuse and Bethlehem have much in common. A young girl at her prayers, as Lewis says, may seem as insignificant as a small light in the night sky or a mustard seed planted in the ground. Yet the closer we look, the greater the wonder and the brighter the glory. The birth of Mary's Son is the greatest event that any of us will ever know, for it represents the planting of God's eternal Word into the soil of our own humanity: "And the word became flesh and dwelt among us, and we have seen his glory" (John 1:14).

The Word that brought into existence the elements, conditions, and natural laws that formed Betelgeuse was born as a baby in Bethlehem because of the belief of a young girl that it could be so. Christmas reminds us that this Word not only forms orange stars of incomprehensible size but also is ready to move heaven to earth if we only have faith the size of a mustard seed or as large as a point of light in the night sky. It simply boggles the mind.

Upside-Down Christmas

God chose what is low and despised in the
world ... to bring to nothing things that are.
—1 Corinthians 1:28

BAOBAB TREES ARE some of the most visually striking
varieties in the world. Their tubular trunks and
root-like branches that grow out of their tops make it
look like their roots are up in the sky. For this reason,
many people call them the "Upside-Down Trees." As a
Christmas present one year, my wife gave me a framed
picture of the Avenue of the Baobabs in Madagascar
at sunset. This picture shows numerous trees lined up
along a dirt road with the light from the west turning
the color of their trunks orange.

Historically, baobab trees have blessed local peoples
in numerous ways. The seeds and pith of the pods are
edible and can be used for medicine; the fibers of the
bark can be made into baskets, nets, and even clothes;

and hollowed-out trunks can be used as shelter. Because of the many uses for the bark, the trunks of baobab trees are often scarred and damaged.[1]

These unusual-looking, scarred trees that appear to be upside down have much to teach us about Christmas. The birth of Jesus was unusual in many ways. He was born in a stable or a cave. He slept in a manger. And many people, including practical shepherds, intellectual wise men, and celestial angels, declared Him to be a king. But none of these things make sense. Everything seems upside down. What king is born and nursed in a cave? What royal baby is placed in a manger normally used to feed animals? Would wise men travel thousands of miles to give expensive and rare gifts to a baby with no noble ancestry? Would shepherds leave their flocks to see a baby born where they normally kept those same animals penned? Would angels fill the sky with praise for an undistinguished couple's firstborn son?

The answer to these questions is that the baby born in Bethlehem is very much like a baobab tree of Madagascar. Like the tree that feeds people with its fruit, Jesus will grow up to say that He is the Bread of Life and those who come to Him will hunger no

---

1. See Thomas Parkenham, *The Remarkable Baobab* (New York: W.W. Norton & Company, 2004).

more (John 6:35–51). Like the tree that heals people with medicine made from its bark, Jesus will move among the people, touch them, and restore their lives (Mark 2:17). Like the tree that provides shelter, Jesus will welcome people to find shelter and rest from the burdens of life in Him (Matthew 11:28–30). And like the tree that is scarred by people who take all these things from it, Jesus will be scarred in His own body so that others might enjoy the blessings He came as a baby in a manger to offer them.

Everything about the birth and ministry of Jesus appears upside down. Christmas forces us to look at the world from a different point of view. It forces us to see how God chose to offer the gift of salvation and life with Him through the birth of a baby in a manger and the death of a man on a cross. The apostle Paul captures this truth in his letter to the Corinthians as he writes that God has used things that are weak, foolish, or upside down for His own purposes, and in this way, He has turned the world downside up (1 Corinthians 1:18–31).

This Christmas, be like the baobab Jesus. Live like the One who came into the world upside down with His roots in heaven so that the world might be turned downside up.

Part Four

Possibility

Day 16

Abraham's Blessing

I will bless those who bless you.
—Genesis 12:3

AN ORANGE COMET flashes across an intensely deep blue sky in Giotto di Bondone's Renaissance-era work of art, *Adoration of the Magi*. The comet streaks over the manger where wise men with golden halos offer gifts to the baby Jesus as His parents, also crowned with golden halos, look on. The painting is a colorful depiction of one of the most enigmatic stories in the Gospels.

A key to the story's meaning lies in the reason Matthew wrote his Gospel in the first place. He wanted to show Jesus to be a son of Abraham. Matthew does this by tracing Jesus' genealogy back to Abraham (Matthew 1:1) and by describing Joseph as a "just man," which relates him to the patriarch (Matthew 1:19). Matthew reports that John the Baptist preaches about Abraham to the Pharisees when he says to them: "Do not presume to say to yourselves, 'We have Abraham as our father,' for I tell you, God is able from these stones to raise up children for Abraham" (Matthew 3:7–10).

Matthew shows Jesus to be a son of Abraham by having Him submit to John's baptism to "fulfill all righteousness," which in the passage means to raise men and women to be children of Abraham (Matthew 3:13–15). He later shows that Abraham is on Jesus' mind when during the Sermon on the Mount Jesus says, "Blessed are those who hunger and thirst for righteousness" (Matthew 5:6); "unless your righteousness exceeds that of the scribes and Pharisees, you will never enter the kingdom of heaven" (Matthew 5:20); "beware of practicing your righteousness before other people" (Matthew 6:1); and "seek first the kingdom of God and his righteousness, and all these things will be added to you" (Matthew 6:33). With each of these references to righteousness, Jesus recalls Abraham, the great example who "believed the Lord, and [the Lord] counted it to him as righteousness" (Genesis 15:6).

In all this, Matthew shows that Jesus is Abraham's son. Through Him, the promise God makes to Abraham to have many descendants (Genesis 15:5) is kept because it is through Him that the gospel will be preached to all nations (Matthew 28:19–20) and those who receive it will experience God's righteousness.

With Matthew's keen interest in Abraham, the story of the wise men takes on fresh meaning. These learned men and star gazers likely came from Abraham's ancestral homeland and were following what they believed to be a sign of God's promise to Abraham based on their studies of the ancient sacred story: "Look toward heaven, and number the stars, if you are able to number them. … So shall your offspring be" (Genesis 15:5). What clearer sign of this promise than that of a star itself? Matthew casts the wise men as those who are seeking after an understanding of the promise of inheritance and blessing God made to one of their ancestors who had traveled centuries earlier on a similar route in his quest for a new home by following a star in the sky.

For Matthew, the gifts the wise men give to Jesus represent the blessing of the nations promised to Abraham: "I will bless those who bless you, … and in you all the families of the earth shall be blessed" (Genesis 12:3). By bringing gifts to the Jesus, the magi blessed Abraham through Him. As they did this, they prepared themselves for the blessing of righteousness that would come to them from that same child who, as a grown man, would die on a cross and extend to them the blessing of an eternal relationship with God.

The star that went before the wise men that first Christmas was a sign to them, even as it is a sign to us today. It is a sign of Abraham's faith and God's gift of righteousness. It is a sign of blessing that issues out of faith and allows all men and women to become sons and daughters of Abraham. This Christmas, receive the blessing of God's righteousness in your life through Abraham's Son Jesus by placing all your faith in Him.

Day 17

Hurrying to Christmas

*And they went with haste and found Mary
and Joseph, and the baby lying in a manger.*
—Luke 2:16

ONE OF THE most popular toys over the past 50 years
has been the die-cast Hot Wheels car made by the
Mattel Corporation. Hundreds of fantastic models
of actual and imaginary cars have brought smiles to
countless boys and girls since the first ones were made
in 1968. As a boy, I was thrilled to receive several Hot
Wheels cars with sections of racing track as a present
one Christmas. I spent hours racing my gold-colored
Custom Volkswagen against my emerald-green Mantis,
the neon-pink Whip Creamer, and the powder-blue
'57 T-Bird over plastic strips of bright orange track. I
raced my favorite, a burnished bronze Custom Firebird,
against all comers, including the blue-green Beach
Bomb. Much of the appeal of the toy cars was the

Spectraflame paint and flashy colors, crazy designs, and wild names given to the cars, as well as the track that could be configured in all kinds of different ways.[1]

Many of us race through Christmas like I used to race my Custom Firebird over the orange track years ago. We fall into our Christmas routines and hurry through the turns and loops of the season, beginning the day after Thanksgiving and not slowing down until after New Year's Day. We speed to stores to buy gifts for friends and loved ones. We rush from house to house to eat calorie-rich foods at Christmas parties. We even race to church to be inspired and reminded of "the reason for the season."

Mary and Joseph were in a hurry that first Christmas too. They were among thousands of people the Roman emperor ordered to return to their hometowns to register for his census. Since they lived in Nazareth to the north, they had to travel about 75 miles to fulfill this duty in Bethlehem. Their journey took about a week, given Mary's pregnancy, and due to her condition, they likely took the road straight south through the Gilboa Mountains, Samarian Hills, and Bethel Hills, rather

---

1. The miniature cars were also designed to roll fast and simulate the drag-racing that was popular in the 1960s. Angelo Van Bogart, *Hot Wheels Classics: The Redline Era* (Iola, WI: Krause Publications, 2009), 16–17.

than the longer route through the Jordan River valley. Despite their reluctance to travel through Samaria, they probably did. It was not an easy trip.

Others were also in a hurry that year. Matthew reports that wise men from Persia sought a newborn king. Traveling some 1,000 miles to Jerusalem, they made the long journey not because of a Roman edict but because of what they perceived to be a heavenly one in the appearance of an unusual star. As men who studied the night sky, they were familiar with the movement of the cosmos and would have moved quickly after the appearance of this particular star. "Where is he who has been born king of the Jews?" they asked King Herod upon their arrival in Jerusalem, "For we saw his star when it rose and have come to worship him" (Matthew 2:2). They had come to give gifts of tribute to the promised King and His family.

Some traveled much shorter distances. Luke writes that local shepherds quickly made their way to Bethlehem from the surrounding hills in response to the angel's promise of salvation. They didn't waste any time: "Let us go over to Bethlehem and see this thing that has happened, which the Lord has made known to us. And they went with haste and found Mary and Joseph, and the baby lying in a manger" (Luke 2:15–16).

The urgency of that first Christmas is matched years later when people hurry after Jesus as He calls,

"Follow me, and I will make you become fishers of men." *Walk a road with Me,* He tells them, *and I will transform your lives' ambition and purpose.* Their responses are decisive. "And immediately they left their nets and followed him." They wanted new purpose and desired to go in a new way (Mark 1:17–18).

Mary and Joseph hurry because of a Roman ruler's decree and because the time of her delivery is close. The wise men hurry to keep up with the star as it moves across the dark sky. And the shepherds make haste to the manger to see the baby born that very night. When Jesus calls His first disciples to walk with Him, they go immediately. Yes, Christmas is the season to hurry, not after last-minute sales or festive get-togethers, but after the One who was born and who even now calls us to follow Him.

For some, the way may be difficult and inconvenient; for others, the way may be long and require patience; and for still others, the way may be short but demand an immediate response. Our roads will take different configurations, like my Hot Wheel tracks did. But whatever God's way is for you this Christmas, make haste after Jesus. Like Mary, experience the miracle of new life. Like the shepherds, look upon the source of your salvation. And like the wise men, bow down before His majesty in worship. Jesus wants to fill your life with meaning and give you purpose. Now is the time.

Day 18

Joseph the Just

And her husband Joseph, being a just man ...
—Matthew 1:19

ONE CHRISTMAS SEASON, my family visited Disneyland where we are told dreams come true. My young son's dreams did come true that day in an unexpected encounter with Tigger outside Cinderella's castle. When the neon-orange storybook character came up and hugged him, the smile that spread across my son's face was pure joy. He could not have been happier; of all the characters in A.A. Milne's *One Hundred Acre Wood*, Tigger was his favorite. Based on the Milne family's black spaniel, "Chum," the bouncing tiger's rambunctious personality so captured my son's imagination that he took to mimicking him in his speech and actions.[1] One day when I corrected something

---

1. Ann Thwaite, *A.A. Milne: The Man behind Winnie-the-Pooh* (New York: Random House, 1990), 123.

he had said, he responded, "Horsefeathers!" (one of Tigger's irreverent expressions) to communicate the frustration he felt.

The birth of Jesus was attended by visions of angels, words of God, and dreams. Mary saw the angel Gabriel while her relative Zechariah had a vision of an angel at the temple. Later, simple shepherds saw a host of God's angels in the night sky over Bethlehem. God not only sent divine messengers, but He also spoke by His Spirit. Old Simeon heard the Holy Spirit announce a Savior at the same time the prophetess Anna heard Him speak about the redemption of Israel. And while all these people saw angels and heard the Spirit, Joseph dreamed dreams.

What kind of man was this dreamer? We're not told much about Joseph in the Gospels, except that he was "a just man and unwilling to put [Mary] to shame" (Matthew 1:19) when he found out about her pregnancy. Joseph the Just is how the apostle Matthew describes this man. By describing him in this way, however, Matthew does not simply mean that Joseph is fair-minded. Instead, he means that Joseph was a man who lived his life as much as possible in obedience to God's ways given in the Torah.[2] He wanted to do the *godly* thing. And as

2. The Greek term *dikaios* is also translated as *righteous*.

Joseph processed all the detritus and horsefeathers of the unwelcome news—how his mind must have roiled with unanswered questions—he fell asleep, and it was then that God spoke to him. What was he to do? God showed Joseph what the *godly* thing to do was in a dream. He was to keep his vow to Mary and name the baby boy *Jesus*, "for he will save his people from their sins" (Matthew 1:21).

After Jesus' birth, Joseph kept dreaming. Months later, when the magi appeared in Jerusalem, Joseph dreamed again. He may have been anxious over Herod's reaction to the appearance of these wise men and the gifts they brought. He may have perceived the danger of having his young son pronounced a king by these foreigners. What was he to do? More horsefeathers. In the swirl of questions and apprehensions, Joseph wanted to do the *godly* thing, and God spoke to him in a dream a second time. He was to take his wife and son and flee to Egypt.

As Joseph walked the Way of the Sea southward with Mary and Jesus, did he think about his biblical namesake? Did he think about the patriarch Joseph who also dreamed dreams and was used to save his family during a time of famine so that they would be able to one day return to their land and fulfill God's purposes for them? Did Joseph remember his first dream and think that God was using him to protect

His Son so that one day He might save God's people from their sins? We can't know his thoughts, but we do know that God spoke to Joseph in yet another dream later to tell him to return to his home after Herod died.

What are you dreaming this year? You may be dreaming with Bing Crosby of a "White Christmas." Or you may be dreaming of giant mice, tin soldiers, and nutcrackers along with Pyotr Ilyich Tchaikovsky.

Children certainly dream of Santa Claus and brightly wrapped presents. If sugarplums are not dancing in their heads, then the latest electronic games are. Without question, Christmas is large enough for all these dreams.

For others, their minds may bear questions that need answers and issues that require resolution. You may find your thoughts filled with horsefeathers. However much you are preoccupied with the *whys* and *hows* and *whats* of life, God wants to speak to you this Christmas as He did to Joseph. For those of us like him who want to do the *godly* thing, God will make His ways known. You can be confident that He will reveal what you are to do and the way you are to go. He may speak through Scripture or the counsel of a trusted friend, or He may speak in a dream as He did to Joseph that first Christmas. Regardless of how God speaks, Christmas is the season for hearing His voice and seeing the *godly* thing done in your life.

Day 19

Jerome's Gift

We have this treasure in jars of clay.
—2 Corinthians 4:7

IN AUGUST 2001, my wife and I traveled to Israel with a church group led by Pastor Jack Hayford. During the ten-day whirlwind of activity, we visited sites throughout the land, beginning with the Upper Room and garden tomb in Jerusalem, continuing to the ancient city of Jericho and the traditional location of the Sermon on the Mount in Galilee, and finishing at the site of ancient Caesarea. Of all these places, the highlight of the trip for me was our visit to Bethlehem and the Church of the Nativity. This stage of the trip remains clear in my memory for reasons other than the weathered beauty of the church or the chance I had to look upon the fourteen-point silver star that marks the place where tradition says Jesus was born.

After our group left the building and congregated outside in the dusty plaza, I was disappointed not to see St. Jerome's Grotto, which was preserved within the church but shut and locked by a gate. The steps down to the cave where we are told the saint translated the Greek and Hebrew books of the Bible into Latin to create the Vulgate were closed. Pastor Jack must have overheard me because he appeared a few minutes later with the priest in charge of the church who said he would open the gates so I might visit the grotto. After he opened them, we walked down worn steps to a small dark cave. He turned on an overhead light and left me in the grotto alone.

As I stood in Jerome's small cell, I thought of the man and the twenty years he gave to translate the Bible into the common language of the people in the early fourth century. I recalled Francisco de Goya's painting of the saint that I show to Greek students each year to inspire them in a light-hearted way to learn the language of the New Testament. In it, de Goya depicts Jerome gazing with yearning at a crucifix that is his inspiration for the work of translation. His face is flush, and he is wearing an orange-colored wrap around his waist. A flagellum lies nearby, and a skull sits on a ledge.[1] Students who have very little in

1. De Goya's portrait of Jerome may be accessed online at norton-simon.org. It is a curious fact that many other portraits of Jerome clothe him in orange as well. Masaccio's *Saints Jerome*

common with Jerome laugh at the thought that they are following in the footsteps of such a man.

His many letters, writings, and translations reveal that Jerome was at once both brilliant and petty, a man who used his ability with words to salve wounds and praise friends as well as to inflict hurts and ridicule opponents. He was stubborn and proud of his classical education and scholarship while, at the same time, insecure and sensitive to criticism and quick to change positions to protect his standing as a man of learning. In all things he strove to live a chaste and devoted life before God and prove himself to be faithful to his Lord. In other words, he was not so very different from you and me. He chose Bethlehem as the place to translate the Bible precisely because it was there Jesus was born and there Jerome's translation work could spread to believers throughout the East and West.[2]

and John the Baptist depicts the church father as wearing a bright orange-red robe and cardinal hat, yet with an exceedingly dour facial expression. Georges de la Tour's St. Jerome Reading (1648), Jusepe de Ribera's St. Jerome and Angel of Judgment, and Pietro Perugino's odd St. Jerome Supporting Two Men on the Gallows are others that show the saint wearing orange-hued vermillion.

2. See Stefan Rebenich, Jerome (The Early Church Fathers) (London: Routledge, 2002), 3–59, for a brief but useful biographical introduction to the saint.

On that hot afternoon in the cool quiet of a small grotto in the Church of the Nativity, I saw for the first time Jerome's translation as an act of Christmas devotion. He had settled in Bethlehem, the birthplace of Christian faith, to labor over what he believed would be a great gift to those who shared his faith. He gave years of his life to develop a gift that has blessed countless believers out of his gratitude for the gift God had given in His Son. The difficult and irascible Jerome teaches all of us that even with all our flaws and foibles, when we give our time and talents to the Lord in gratitude for what He has given to us, we celebrate Him who was born on Christmas Day.

Day 20

Keys to the Grotto

I will give you the keys of the kingdom of heaven.

—Matthew 16:19

As I STOOD in St. Jerome's cell in Bethlehem that hot summer afternoon, I thought about the keys that had been used to open the gates for me. Not the keys used by the priest from the large metal ring in his hands, but the unseen ones possessed by Pastor Jack Hayford. By that time, he had taken more than 30 church and study groups to Israel, and today, this number has increased to more than 40 such groups. Through those trips, Pastor Jack has nurtured a trust and bond with numerous Christian and Jewish leaders over the years. Such was the confidence that the custodians of the Church of the Nativity had in him that they were willing to unlock the gates and open them to me so that I could visit the site. They didn't know me, of course, but they knew Pastor Jack. And it was because of his willingness to intercede for me to see Jerome's grotto for myself that the gates swung open and I found myself standing in the middle of it.

One day as Jesus and His disciples were passing through Caesarea Philippi, He asked who people said He was. The disciples replied, "Some say John the Baptist, others say Elijah, and others Jeremiah or one of the prophets" (Matthew 16:14). Jesus wanted to know what the disciples thought, so Peter spoke up and said, "You are the Christ, the Son of the living God." Matthew reports that Jesus enthusiastically responds to Peter's answer by saying that he is blessed because only God his Father could have given him this insight. Jesus reacts with joy because Peter confirms the word that Jesus first heard Himself when He was baptized at the Jordan River: "You are my beloved son" (Mark 1:11). The revelation Jesus received then has now been given by God to one of His disciples.

Jesus says to Peter, "Upon this rock I will build my church. ... I will give you the keys of the kingdom of heaven" (Matthew 16:18–19). Though different church traditions claim that the rock to which Jesus refers is Peter himself or Peter's faith, the rock is the revelatory word that Peter has just spoken to Jesus. This point becomes clear when we look at the conclusion to the Sermon on the Mount where Jesus tells His disciples that if they build their lives upon the rock of His teaching, the storms of life will not overthrow them: "And the rain fell, and the floods came, and the winds blew and beat on that house, but it did not fall, because it had been founded on the rock" (Matthew 7:25). There the rock is the revelatory teaching of Jesus given to the disciples in the sermon. When Jesus says that the Church will be built upon the rock and the gates of hell will not prevail against it, He means the same revelatory word of God which this time has been spoken through Peter. The Church will be built upon the word that God reveals to us.

Jesus goes on to tell Peter that the Church also will possess the keys of the kingdom. Since Jesus is the King of the kingdom, the keys represent the authority by which He rules. And the authority He shows on earth is the power of the Holy Spirit. The expression "keys of the kingdom" refers to the Spirit of God. Jesus will send the Spirit to the Church so that the rule of God will be done on earth as it is in heaven. In this passage, Matthew shows that, according to Jesus, it is by the word of God and the Spirit of God that the people of God will stand and carry out His purposes in the world. And all of this is possible because of the new level of relationship Peter has with Jesus as indicated by the new name Jesus gives to him: "Simon Bar-Jonah" or "Simon son of Jonah" (Matthew 16:17).

Very few Jewish families would have named their sons "Jonah" because of the negative attitude they had toward the prophet at that time. Of all the Old Testament prophets, Jonah is the one who refused to speak God's message when God wanted it spoken. He had to be swallowed by a fish and spat up on a beach before he would fulfill his mission. Even then Jonah was unhappy and unwilling to do what God wanted. Peter's father was not named Jonah. So what does Jesus mean by calling him this?

According to Matthew, the Pharisees approached Jesus on more than one occasion. They wanted Him to perform a sign for them, likely for the purpose of gathering evidence against Him to show Him to be a false prophet. Jesus refuses and says on two occasions that the only sign He will give will be the sign of Jonah (Matthew 12:38–41, 16:1–4). This sign is His death and resurrection. Just as Jonah was swallowed by a fish only to be given new life when he was thrown up on the beach, so also Jesus will be put to death and raised to life. He is the new Jonah, and by confessing Jesus to be the Messiah, the Son of the living God, Peter is His son. Peter enters into a new relationship with Jesus as a result of the revelatory word God gave to him, and because of that word, he will see God's purposes fulfilled in his life with the help of the Spirit.

KEYS TO THE GROTTO | 95

God's revealed word is the foundation for our lives in the midst of life's storms. His Spirit is the means by which we will fulfill His plans here on earth. That afternoon in Bethlehem, I saw how the keys of the kingdom work. Jack Hayford possessed the authority to have the gates of the Church of the Nativity opened as a result of his relationship with its caretakers, and I possessed a relationship with Pastor Jack. Through him, I saw the gates of Jerome's grotto opened wide for me. Jesus said that the Spirit will be given to His followers as they live in relationship with Him so that they might experience the kingdom and see its possibilities manifested in their lives.

The One whose birthplace is marked by the Church of the Nativity came into the world to offer a new life with God. He came so we might enjoy the presence of His Spirit and experience the blessings of His kingdom—His rule—in our lives. This season, the Holy Spirit wants to unlock the gates of opportunity and purpose in God's kingdom that we could never enter or see otherwise. He wants to swing open the gates to those things that have been closed to us and lead us into His realm of purpose and opportunity. Are we ready? In joy, let us take hold of the keys of the kingdom that Jesus offers this Christmas and enter into a world of divine possibilities.

Part Five

Destiny

Day 21

Glory!

Glory to God in the highest.

–Luke 2:14

ONE OF THE most beloved Christmas singles of all time is Nat King Cole's "The Christmas Song." Most people know the lyrics and can sing from memory about roasting chestnuts and the cold of Jack Frost. Cole's daughter Natalie left her own mark on the music of the season by dubbing her voice with that of her father on a later remake of the song. She is also known for her memorable rendition of "My Grown-Up Christmas List," written by David Foster, which expresses the desire for universal friendship, justice, and love.

The winner of numerous awards, Natalie Cole is most known for singing soft-jazz contemporary songs. Of these, none is more fun than "Orange Colored Sky," written by Milton DeLugg and Willie Stein. This song breezily describes the heart-stopping moment when she sees Mr. Right. It is hard not to smile while listening to her sing about unexpectedly meeting her new love like a flash out of an orange-colored sky.

This love song was popular when first released for its melody and catchy lines and for the fact that many people could identify with that love-struck moment when they saw someone for the first time. Part of the effectiveness of the lyrics lies in their irony and the fact that they are most often used to describe an unexpected and unwelcomed event in our lives. An unanticipated financial setback, an unexpected medical report, or a crisis in the family can bury us under anxiety and fear, which then send us into a freefall by removing the security we thought was under us. For the ceiling to fall in or the bottom to fall out normally speaks of disaster or ruin. This song takes that expression of calamity and uses it to describe unexpected fortune and joy.

On the first Christmas night, the ceiling of heaven fell in upon a traumatized world. When the angels declared the birth of "a Savior, who is Christ the Lord" (Luke 2:11), the bottom of loss, need, and ignorance fell out. All those who looked upon Jesus that night were witnesses to the collapse of the ceiling of heavenly possibility upon a suffering world and the collapse of the floor of human impossibility under its weight.

Famous British author J.R.R. Tolkien describes this collapse as a "'eucatastrophe': the sudden happy turn in a story which pierces you with a joy that brings tears."[1] The angels proclaimed this *eucatastrophe* as they sang, "Glory to God in the highest, and on earth peace among those with whom he is pleased" (Luke 2:14). Glory, peace, and God's pleasure all descended upon the earth that first Christmas because of a Child the prophet Isaiah had already named "Wonderful Counselor" (Isaiah 9:6).

This Christmas may feel as if the ceiling has fallen in upon you and the bottom fallen out from beneath. You may feel as though you are covered with failure or that you're standing on floorboards about to give way to disaster. Such feelings are very real. But if you look carefully toward Bethlehem, you will see that the sky is colored orange. You will see that the ceiling of heaven has fallen in upon you, God's wonderful Son has come near to you, and the floor of impossibility has collapsed below you. There is nothing else for you to say to these amazing things except Glory! Hallelujah!

---

1. "The Resurrection was the greatest 'eucatastrophe' possible in the greatest Fairy Story—and produces that essential emotion: Christian joy which produces tears because it is qualitatively so like sorrow, because it comes from those places where Joy and Sorrow are at one, reconciled, as selfishness and altruism are lost in Love." J.R.R. Tolkien, Humphrey Carpenter, and Christopher Tolkien, *The Letters of J.R.R. Tolkien* (New York: Houghton Mifflin Harcourt, 2000), 100-101.

Day 22

Return from Exile

You are the light of the world.
—Matthew 5:14

ONE YEAR I decided to unscrew all the orange bulbs
from our strands of outdoor Christmas lights and
replace them with other colors. I reasoned that green
and red are Christmas colors, not *orange*. After I had
removed the bulbs from the strands and replaced them
with what I thought were more appropriate ones, I
stood back to behold my work. Even when I moved
my head to one side and squinted my eyes, the strands
didn't look right. They didn't look as festive as before,
so I unscrewed the green and red replacement bulbs
and returned the original orange ones.

When Joseph and Mary arrived in Bethlehem,
they couldn't find a place to stay. They were miles
from home with nowhere to rest. Later, they fled to
Egypt when King Herod tried to purge the region

around Bethlehem of all young boys after hearing the wise men's story. Did the thought cross Mary's and Joseph's minds as they traveled that they were reliving the experience of their forefathers? Their earliest ancestors had gone into Egypt while others had been scattered by the Assyrians, and yet others were uprooted and planted far away in Babylon. Like those before them, they were experiencing exile. They were like bulbs removed from the strand of their homeland and people.

Jesus' life was one of exile, too. Not only was He born in a stable far from his parents' home, but once in the midst of his ministry, He was approached by a scribe who boasted that he would follow Jesus wherever he went. "Foxes have holes, and birds of the air have nests," Jesus said to him, "but the Son of Man has nowhere to lay his head" (Matthew 8:19–20). After Jesus was executed on the cross, Joseph of Arimathea took His body and placed it in Joseph's own tomb since Jesus' family didn't have one. No room for Jesus at His birth, no place to rest during His ministry, and no family burial at His death. No place on the world's strand for the one John describes as the Light of the World.

Jesus also experienced social exile because of the unusual nature of His birth. Neighbors and relatives wondered about His legitimacy and called him "the son of Mary" (Mark 6:1–6). Jesus should have been known as "the son of Joseph," whether or not Joseph was still living. No young man at that time would have been identified as the son of his mother unless it was to demean him. The people hadn't forgotten the story of Jesus' birth and in their minds continued to think of Him as Mary's son—not Joseph's. They had removed Him from the strand of kinship and relationship, and their attitude hindered Jesus from performing any miracles in their midst.

This negative attitude was shared by temple leaders, according to John. In an acrimonious debate with them concerning sin and righteousness, Jesus questioned their claim to be sons of Abraham and said, "If you were Abraham's children, you would be doing the works Abraham did, but now you seek to kill me." Their harsh response questioned Jesus' own ancestry: "We were not born of sexual immorality. We have one Father—even God" (John 8:31–59). In other words, the leaders accused Jesus of being born illegitimately and having no position to talk to them about their ancestry when He doesn't even know His own. The abrasive exchange ends with the leaders attempting to stone Jesus. In their minds, He has no place in their strand of religious faith, and they want to remove Him from it.

For those of us who have experienced any kind of rejection or exile, the Christmas story is one of our return. Jesus knows what it is like to be removed from the strand of one's family and friends. He knows what it is like for people to say, "You don't belong," and because He knows these things, He says to us this Christmas, "Come to me, all who labor and are heavy laden, and I will give you rest. Take my yoke upon you, and learn from me, for I am gentle and lowly in heart, and you will find rest for your souls" (Matthew 11:28–29).

Because we have all labored under the judgment of others and borne the yoke of labels that people have placed on us, Christmas is about welcome and acceptance. It is also about having a home with Jesus so that God might reflect His glory through us. Christmas is the end of our exile as Jesus returns us to our places in the strand of God's people to be lights for all the world to see. Christmas is our time to shine.

Day 23

God's Gift of Change

*Every good gift and every perfect gift
is from above.*

—James 1:17

MY PATERNAL GRANDPARENTS were far ahead of the curve when it came to Christmas trees. They had their first artificial one sometime in the 1960s. But theirs was not a Martha Stewart White Pine dusted with flakes of faux snow; it was a four-foot silver aluminum tree with pink bulbs and looked like it came off the lot in *A Charlie Brown Christmas*. There was everything pretentious about their tree. It shouted, "Commercial!" It sang, "Artificial!" It shimmered. It dazzled. But the most magical quality about their tree was that it changed color. One moment it was blue, the next red, another yellow, and then green. It even turned *orange*. The rotating color wheel behind the tree had a light that shone through the pie-shaped plastic pieces and transformed it into a rainbow. It mesmerized all of us grandchildren.

The silver tree and its color wheel taught us in a flashy way that Christmas is about *change*. It is about the transformation that God wants to work in all of our lives through the light of His Son. Of course, no one experienced greater transformation that first Christmas morning than Mary. There was nothing subtle about the angel or his message. The power of the Most High would overshadow her, and she would become a living tabernacle for the eternal God.[1] Mary was changed into a sacred place of worship, and from that moment on, she always lived with the treasure of God's Word in her heart.

Joseph's life was changed, too, and he would never be the same. He became the father of a Son without fathering a son. People questioned his judgment when he wed Mary, and he endured the whispers of family and friends. Joseph bore the shame that they imposed upon him in a culture where honor held the highest value.[2] Yet along with this responsibility came

1. The word *overshadow* in Luke 1:35 translates *episkiazō*, which is the same word found in Exodus 40:35 of the Greek Septuagint to describe the settling of the cloud over the tabernacle in the wilderness.
2. David deSilva describes the way that honor and shame defined Jewish culture at the time of Jesus in his book, *Honor, Patronage, Kinship & Purity: Unlocking New Testament Culture* (Downers Grove: IVP Academic, 2000), 23-93.

the privilege of naming God's Son: "You shall call his name Jesus, for he will save his people from their sins" (Matthew 1:21). God gave Joseph a sacred vocation and a new purpose in life.

The shepherds were never the same either. The appearance of the heavenly host forever changed their outlook on the world. Over their heads, they had heard music in the air and would always remember the lyrics: "Glory to God in the highest, and on earth peace among those with whom he is pleased!" (Luke 2:14).[3] Beginning that night, they became singers of the sacred song of good news to all people and the birth of the long-awaited Davidic king.

The wise men were changed by their weeks-long journey to Judea as well. Their ideas of wisdom and power were forever transformed by the Son of a young Jewish couple. None of their charts, maps, or books of philosophy could explain the miracle of the star that had guided them. And nothing could explain the divine direction they were given in a dream afterward. They were changed by the discovery that wisdom is not hidden in the stars of the sky but is present in the birth of a Bethlehem boy.

---

3. This wording is borrowed from the African American spiritual that is as simple as it is memorable: "Over my head I hear music in the air. There must be a God somewhere."

That first Christmas changed the lives of all these people. We learn from their experiences that Christmas is about being people of worship who treasure God's Word and who have a sacred vocation. It is about singing a new song and thinking in a new way. Their stories remind us of the new things God desires to bring into each of our lives through His Son.

Just as my grandparents' Christmas tree changed colors because of the light from the wheel that shone on it, we are changed by the light of God's living Word. James writes, "Every good gift and every perfect gift is from above, coming down from the Father of lights, with whom there is no variation or shadow due to change" (James 1:17). God doesn't change, but the light that He gives in His Son is a gift that will change us. This Christmas, open the gift from above in Jesus so that your worship of God, purpose in life, and outlook on the world might be changed and dazzle all who see Him in you.

Day 24

Nicodemus' Christmas

I am the light of the world. Whoever follows me will not walk in darkness but will have the light of life.

—John 8:12

MANY PEOPLE CELEBRATE Christmas by making Christingles and giving them as gifts to friends and family. A Christingle is an orange wrapped in red ribbon with a small candle and pieces of dried fruit stuck to it with toothpicks.[1] I remember thinking how much it looked like a model of a space satellite the first time I saw one. Despite its Jet Propulsion Laboratory appearance, the symbolism of the Christingle is easy to grasp. The orange represents the world, and the candle is Jesus, the light of the world. The red ribbon symbolizes Jesus'

1. John de Watteville came up with the idea for Christingles in nineteenth century Germany and introduced them into his Moravian Christmas Eve services.

blood shed for the forgiveness of sins, and the pieces of fruit are the four seasons of the year. Altogether, this curious ornament is a symbol of God's love for all people all the time through Jesus the light of the world.

John's Gospel gives a Christingle version of the Christmas story. He doesn't describe the birth of a baby born in a manger in Bethlehem. He doesn't say anything about singing angels or wondering shepherds. He doesn't mention shining stars or ancient astronomers. Instead, John describes a Word spoken at the beginning of time, full of life, and best imagined as light for the whole world. He says this Word of life and light became flesh and lived with us (John 1:4–14).

John then recounts the story of Nicodemus meeting with Jesus. Nicodemus approaches Jesus in the dark of night to ask about God's kingdom (John 3:1–21). This teacher of Israel, as Jesus calls him, wants to learn more from the miracle-working Rabbi. The good He is doing means that God is with Him—*Immanuel* in the words of Isaiah—but Jesus is also doing things that don't make any sense and can't be condoned, like overturning tables in the temple (John 2:13–22). Nicodemus is confused and approaches Jesus in the darkness of his confusion, seeking the light of understanding.

Jewish teachers such as Nicodemus believed that references to light in Scripture were symbolic of God's

presence and divine knowledge. He knew the story of
the Exodus, in which God appeared as light to Israel as
He led them through the wilderness. Nicodemus knew,
too, from Isaiah that God appeared as light to His
people later in the time of exile:

> "The people who walked in darkness
> 　　have seen a great light;
> those who dwelt in a land of deep darkness,
> 　　on them has light shined" (Isaiah 9:2).

He also knew from that same book that Israel was to
be a light to the Gentiles just as God had been a light to
them:

> "I will give you as a covenant for the people,
> 　　a light for the nations,
> 　　to open eyes that are blind,
> to bring out the prisoners from the dungeon,
> from the prison those who sit in darkness"
> 　　(Isaiah 42:6–7).

Though Nicodemus initially approaches Jesus
in doubt and confusion, he doesn't remain in the
darkness. John reports that Nicodemus later defends
Jesus before his Pharisaic colleagues and urges them
to listen to Jesus' teachings. Nicodemus wants them
to see the light that he is beginning to see. Even later,
after the crucifixion, he and Joseph of Arimathea take

Jesus' body down from the cross and anoint it for burial despite the danger involved in such actions.

Nicodemus celebrated his own Christmas by moving toward God's light in Jesus, the divine Word of life that had become flesh. Nicodemus rejoiced in discerning God's great love for Israel and His marvelous ways for the nations in God's Son.

We are all like Nicodemus at times. We can't make sense of the things happening around us and can't see a clear way ahead. We have more questions than answers and are beset with doubts. A "Nicodemus' Christmas" means that we discover the light that leads us out of our own dark places of ignorance and confusion into new ones of understanding and clarity. It is to see the way forward in our lives, our families, our jobs, and our service to others by looking to the example and instruction that Jesus gives. This Christmas, follow the example of that learned Pharisee and seek out the Light that gives understanding to the world.

Day 25

God's Christmas Way

I am the way, and the truth, and the life.
—John 14:6

THE AMERICAN MUSIC icon Frank Sinatra is remembered today for his winning smile, outgoing personality, and one-of-a-kind singing voice. His most famous quote, "Orange is the happiest color," captures the spirit of the man: surprising, optimistic, and confident. He is known for his many hit songs, including "Fly Me to the Moon," "New York, New York," and Christmas standards like "Have Yourself a Merry Little Christmas." The most famous of all his songs in the minds of many people is "My Way," a ballad that celebrates a life lived free of doubt and with few regrets.

Ultimately, "My Way" attributes the doubt-free, few-regrets kind of life to living true to oneself. It declares that at the end of the day, when we look back over the years of our lives, the one thing we can say with confidence is that we have ourselves.

There is much to embrace in the song's message; self-reliance, determination, commitment, and ambition are all qualities that serve us well in our lives. Nonetheless, we cannot listen to the lyrics of the song without wondering if the way to a regret-free life is achieved through self-reliance. Does a life in which we trust only ourselves lead to a life free from remorse and shame?

Regret speaks of loss, and who among us has not experienced loss of one kind or another? We all have experienced lost relationships, lost opportunities, and even lost dreams. All of us have taken missteps in our lives and lost our way. We have made commitments that we have not kept. We have acted with the best of intentions, only to see those intentions backfire on us. Our missteps, broken commitments, and failed intentions can leave us remorseful and unhappy with more questions than answers. The truth is that many of us look back over our lives and feel twinges of regret over one thing or another.

The wonder of Christmas is that when God looked upon our human condition and saw the path we were walking, He joined Himself to us and went our way. He came alongside us in His Son Jesus so that we could live our lives free from regrets over the past, doubts about the present, and despair concerning our future. The apostle John writes that God came to us to light our way: "The Word became flesh and dwelt among us, and we have seen his glory, glory as of the only Son from the Father, full of grace and truth" (John 1:14). Jesus says, "I will never leave you nor forsake you" (Hebrews 13:5). God came to show us the way out of remorse and shame, not by pointing out the way but by becoming our way. He is with us, and He is our way. This is why John also writes that as Jesus shared a meal with His disciples before His death on the cross, He declared, "I am the way, and the truth, and the life" (John 14:6).

Christmas is the season to let His way become your way. It is to find the answer to life's questions in the One whose birth we celebrate during this season. It is to hear Jesus say to us, "You have yourself in Me, who is the way to the Father. You have yourself in Me, who is the truth that dispels all doubt. And you have yourself in Me, who is the life that is free of regret." Christmas is the happiest season because it is the time when we are reminded that we truly have found ourselves in the baby born in Bethlehem who has become the way for us.

Conclusion

Orange Christmas

MANY OF US think that color is a property of material objects. We think Santa has a big, cherry-red nose because the frosty air causes blood to rush to the surface of his skin and mistletoe is green because of the chlorophyll in its tiny leaves. Silver bells are brilliant because of the elements of the precious metal from which they are made. Science tells us that color is not an intrinsic quality of the things that make up our world but rather of light that shines all around us. Color is present in light and is a quality of the wavelengths of light. Some are short and others long, and they are absorbed by objects that have corresponding short and long wavelengths. The wavelengths of light not absorbed are reflected back into space. It is these that we see with our eyes as *color*.[1]

---

1. Philip Ball points out that there are several causes for our perception of color. See *Bright Earth*, 26–30, 42–45.

What does the light absorbed in oranges stuffed in old socks and pomander balls tell us about Christmas? What can we learn about the Nativity from the Spirit of Christmas Present or the oranges given as gifts today in memory of St. Nicholas' generosity? Is there anything to be learned about the light of God's kingdom in the world from St. Jerome's orange robe painted by Francisco de Goya? Can my little girl's gift of a signed baseball or her favorite Christmas story about a little bird who gives away an orange vest shed light on the birth of Jesus? The reminiscences and reflections given above have attempted to answer these questions with yes.

How can *orange* be the color of Christmas? It is seeing the extraordinary in the ordinary and marveling that heaven has bent low to earth. It is seeing the miraculous in the mundane. But it is also more than this. It is to act upon this vision and give to others just as the God of Israel gave His Son for an impoverished world and St. Nicholas gave small bags of gold to a needy family. It is giving in secret out of a heart that wants to bless and is willing to risk the reward that God will give. It is to say yes along with a young Jewish girl to the astounding promise that God offers to us as well as the daunting responsibilities that come with that promise.

The gifts that surround the tree of an Orange Christmas should cause us to jump and shout like children on Christmas morning. There is the gift of freedom and adoption into God's family. We have been made sons and daughters whereas we were once slaves. For this reason, we have been invited to a Christmas banquet that God has prepared for us in His Son and have been led to an honored place at His table. We have been given an autograph that cannot be priced and a new vest of color to wear for all eternity.

These presents are scattered about the strangest of all Christmas trees. No lights or ornaments brighten it. No tinsel or bulbs hang from it. It stands bare and unadorned. It is a mystery. There is but one light that shines upon it, and it is called the Light of the World. Orange Christmas looks in reverence upon the One who was pierced and hung on that tree for us so that we might be preserved from the moths of life that would quietly and surreptitiously destroy us. It runs to the pure light of that tree in the midst of our darkness because that tree stands as the end of our exile. But how can this be? Is it possible that the greatest thing in the entire universe is the faith of a young girl in the words of angels?

Because of the gifts that are under the tree, Orange Christmas hurries to Bethlehem. It is filled with expectancy and hope in the midst of uncertainty and hardship. It is a walk of faith that follows Jesus from the manger to the cross and into the present. Once we arrive, Orange Christmas will not let us remain the same. The Father of Lights who does not change insists that we be transformed into the image of His Son. He wants to give us dreams like Joseph and understanding like Nicodemus. God wants us to shine as lights in the world because it is His ambition for every one of us, despite our all-too-human frailties and failures, to participate in His kingdom. And to make this possible, He holds out to us a key from His ring—He offers His Spirit—so that we might open the doors of earth to the possibilities of heaven.

John writes that at the birth of Jesus, light was shining in the darkness. In fact, the light was Jesus Himself. As the Light of the World has been absorbed into our hearts and has changed us, let us reflect color back into the world for all to see. This Christmas, let others see the color orange. Let them see the humility and love of the Light that has penetrated our hearts. Let them behold the abundance and commensality of our God in us. Most of all, let them marvel at the greatest mystery in the universe: a man or woman who has been born for a second time and re-made into the very image of God because of the birth of a baby in Bethlehem.

About the Author

JON HUNTZINGER, PHD, is Distinguished Professor of Bible and Ministry at The King's University where he has served since the founding of the school. During that time, he has taught classes in New Testament, biblical Greek and Hebrew, Christian theology, and discipleship. He has also worked as the dean of students, dean of graduate studies, and director of the TKU campus in Los Angeles. While in LA, he and his family were members of The Church On The Way, and he served as an assisting minister there.

Jon is coeditor of the New Testament notes for the *New Spirit-Filled Life Bible* (Thomas Nelson) and author of the commentary on *John* for the *Spirit-Filled Life Commentary Series* (Thomas Nelson). His other writings include *Sinai in the Sanctuary: A Mountain Theology* (Gateway Academic/TKU Press) and *The Trees Will Clap their Hands: A Garden Theology*. In addition, he is coeditor of a book of essays honoring

Jack W. Hayford entitled *The Pastor and the Kingdom* (Gateway Academic/TKU Press, 2017).

Jon enjoys taking walks with his wife, Penney, to whom he has been married for 33 years. They have two grown children, both graduates of Baylor University. They attend Gateway Church in the Dallas/Fort Worth Metroplex, Texas where he teaches in Gateway's Equip program (equip.gatewaypeople.com).

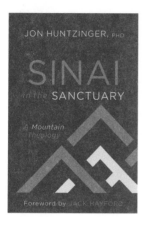